Sea Kayaking
the Carolinas

OTHER TITLES AVAILABLE FROM OUT THERE PRESS

Sea Kayaking Florida & the Georgia Sea Islands

Guides to Backcountry Travel & Adventure

Arkansas (9/98)

North Carolina

South Carolina

Tennessee (7/98)

Virginia

West Virginia

Sea Kayaking
the Carolinas

James Bannon
&
Morrison Giffen

Out There Press
Asheville, North Carolina

Sea Kayaking the Carolinas

Out There Press
P.O. Box 1173
Asheville, NC 28802

Maps drawn by James Bannon

Library of Congress Catalog Card Number: 97-65863
ISBN: 0–9648584–3–6

The authors and publisher have made every effort to ensure the accuracy of the information contained in this book. Nevertheless, they can not be held liable for any loss, damage, injury, or inconvenience sustained by any person using this book. Readers should keep in mind that by its very nature sea kayaking contains elements of risk and danger. In other words, you're on your own out there. Be careful.

Cover photograph and design: James Bannon

Manufactured in the United States

10 9 8 7 6 5 4 3 2

This book is dedicated to all the individuals and organizations who work to preserve the natural habitats in the coastal regions of North and South Carolina

Table of Contents

Map Symbols

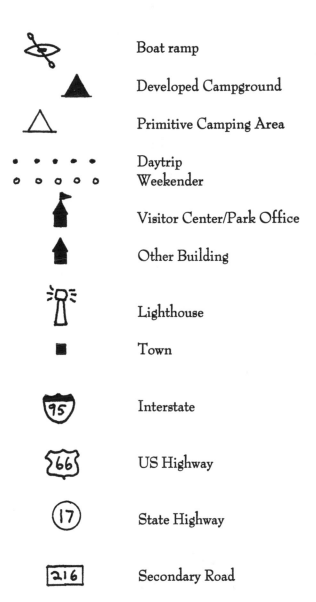

Boat ramp

Developed Campground

Primitive Camping Area

Daytrip
Weekender

Visitor Center/Park Office

Other Building

Lighthouse

Town

Interstate

US Highway

State Highway

Secondary Road

Abbreviations

4WD	Four Wheel Drive
E	east
ERR	Estuarine Research Reserve
ICW	Intracoastal Waterway
L	left
N	north
NPS	National Park Service
NS	National Seashore
NWR	National Wildlife Refuge
R	right
S	south
SNA	State Natural Area
SP	State Park
SRA	State Recreation Area
W	west
WMA	Wildlife Management Area

Introduction

The coastal regions of North and South Carolina offer a paradise to sea kayakers. Covering almost 500 miles between Virginia and Georgia, this stretch of the south Atlantic coast tempts paddlers with an amazing diversity of natural settings. Vast stretches of undeveloped beach, estuaries, and saltwater and freshwater marsh have been protected as national seashores, national wildlife refuges, state parks, and other wilderness preserves. Of the 500 miles of national seashore in the United States, for example, a full one-quarter are located in North Carolina alone. And more than fifty percent of the South Carolina coast is protected in one form or another. The famed string of barrier islands that have been attracting visitors to the region for decades make for some of the most exciting sea kayaking on the East Coast.

While the populations of North and South Carolina continue to increase as people move here from other parts of the country, visitors unfamiliar with the coastal region will be amazed at just how empty most of it still is. A combination of factors—government protection and an extremely dynamic topography chief among them—has spared most of this region from the hyper development that plagues other popular beach areas. The vast undeveloped tracts of the natural environments that characterize the coastal plain—barrier islands, estuaries, marshes, maritime forests, swamp forests, and blackwater rivers—provide vital habitat for an amazing diversity of wildlife.

Located along the Atlantic Flyway, the Carolinas' coastal plain is year-round or part-time home to more than 400 species of birds. These include raptors, waterfowl, shore birds, wading birds, and song birds. Their numbers draw bird watchers from all over to the coast of the Carolinas. A sea kayak is an ideal craft for identifying and observing many of these birds undisturbed in their native habitats. Less visible, but no less numerous, are the dozens of species of fish that roam the offshore and inshore waters of the Carolinas. Strap a rod and reel to your kayak and you're ready for a combined paddling/angling trip.

In addition to the unspoiled natural scenery and native flora and fauna, a handful of attractive waterfront cities that date back to colonial times offer paddlers the chance to explore a slice of American history from a unique perspective. Cities such as Charleston, Georgetown, and Edenton grew up as important ports of entry before the American Revolution. Today they combine vibrant waterfront districts with preservation of their historic heritage. Convenient waterfront access makes it easy to plan a trip that combines paddling their harbors with exploring their many land-based offerings.

With so many different environments to explore, and with bodies of water that include ocean, sounds, lakes, and rivers, the Carolinas entice sea kayakers with a seemingly endless variety of new places to discover. We hope you'll find the locations and trips we've included a useful overview to this exciting region.

Climate

The coastal regions of North and South Carolina enjoy a climate that ranges from temperate to sub-tropical. In addition to its southern location, the major factor that moderates the weather is the location of the Gulf Stream just off the coast of both states. This results in cooling breezes during summer and warms the air during winter, when temperatures along the coast remain approximately 10° higher than inland on the piedmont.

With 500 miles of coast stretching from Virginia to Georgia, there is inevitably a noticeable range in the temperatures along the

Carolina's coast. As you would expect, temperatures increase as you move south. Weather tables at the introduction to each of the two states of show air and water temperatures and wind speed in mph and prevailing direction. Wind speeds vary considerably depending on location. They are strongest on the Outer Banks and at the capes. In those areas where the coast lies on an east-west axis, winds are usually relatively light.

Weather

The weather along the coasts of the Carolinas is a study in contrasts. While sunny pleasant days are certainly the norm for most of the year, they are punctuated every now and then by storms as intense and destructive as any in the nation. From May to October, these include tropical storms and the occasional hurricane. In late fall and winter, the wind shifts direction and blows out of the northeast; severe storms during this period are known as Nor'easters.

For coastal kayakers, air and water temperature, as well as wind speed and direction, are major concerns. Each of these factors will have an impact on any given trip. Before setting out, you should apprise yourself of the current conditions and forecast for your destination. For trips longer than a day, a weather radio should be considered an essential item, particularly during hurricane season. A weather chart showing air temperature, water temperature, wind speed, and prevailing wind direction is located at the start of each of the two main sections in this book.

Tides & Current

In addition to the weather, the other factors with the greatest impact on paddling conditions are the lunar tides and prevailing currents.

Most of the trips covered in this book travel on bodies of water affected by tides. Tidal ranges along the coast of the Carolinas vary from less than two feet to more than six. While this level of rise and fall is not especially dramatic, you can ease your trip by timing it to coincide with the ebb and flow of the tides. In other words, try to paddle toward the ocean on an ebb tide, and back in toward the mainland on a flood tide. This can add from one to two miles per hour to your rate of travel. An exception to this rule is when traveling through an inlet between two bodies of water. The often strong, treacherous currents found at these locations are best navigated during a slack tide, i.e. the time when the tide is changing direction. Tide tables are available for free at most marine and fishing supply stores on the coast.

In addition to currents caused by the lunar tide cycle, several other types of currents are encountered on the coast of the Carolinas. River currents move from inland bodies of freshwater to the ocean. Due to the flat topography of the coastal plain, these currents are typically quite mild. Where the rivers eventually flow into the ocean through narrow inlets, however, is frequently the site of strong, unstable, and conflicting currents. Only skilled kayakers should attempt to navigate these waters. Strong ocean currents, running both parallel and perpendicular to shore, vary considerably depending on location.

When to Go

Sea kayaking is possible year round in the Carolinas. Although there are four distinct seasons, even winters are relatively mild. Spring and fall are probably the most enjoyable seasons for paddling, with comfortable temperatures, fewer visitors to the region than in summer, and moderate numbers of insects. Summer brings crowds to the beach areas, but warm water and pleasant ocean breezes turn sea kayaking into a fun water sport when surfing to shore or practicing rolls is enjoyable rather than an unwelcome necessity. Keep in mind that the intensity of mosquitoes and other biting insects is highest from May to October. Insect repellent is an absolute essential during these months and some areas are best left alone altogether during this period. Paddling conditions change most dramatically during the winter. This can be the most satisfying time of year to paddle, with isolation virtually guaranteed and boat traffic reduced to a handful of fishermen. It is also potentially the most dangerous and therefore requires additional safety precautions on the part of the kayaker. With water temperatures hovering around 50° and cold air and brisk wind often added to the mix, a strategy for getting warm and dry in the event of a capsize or other mishap is essential. Paddling during winter is certainly worth the extra effort; it's the best season for observing the annual migration of birds, and daytime temperatures in the 60°s or even 70°s are not uncommon.

Kayak Touring

For centuries, sea kayaks have provided travellers with a means of reaching otherwise inaccessible areas of wilderness. A kayak's natural stealth and shallow draft make it ideal for exploring sensitive coastal environments. Unlike motor boats, kayaks permit travel through wildlife habitats without disturbing or causing undue stress to the native species. And unlike backpacking, it permits you to carry the gear required for backcountry camping without having to shoulder the load yourself. With an average rate of speed of between 3 and 4 miles per hour, a kayak allows you to cover as many as 30 miles of travel in a day. Rates of travel and distances covered will of course depend on a number of factors, including tides, currents, wind, paddling technique, and your personal level of endurance. All but a few of the trips described in this book cover fewer than 20 miles per day.

What to Bring

What you bring with you on any given paddling trip will depend on several factors: destination, length of trip, time of year, and weather. When preparing a packing list for a trip, include whatever you'll need for the worst conditions you're likely to encounter. While this may seem like a pessimistic way of looking forward to a paddling trip, it will also ensure that you're never caught unprepared, and practically guarantees that your trip won't unexpectedly turn unpleasant or worse.

Below are three lists of things you should have with you when kayaking: safety items, daytrip items, and camping trip items. Items in the first two lists should be considered essentials. Items included under camping trips are in addition to those listed under daytrip items. The kayak supply stores listed in the appendix at the back of this book can provide you with supplies and offer suggestions. Many of the items are also available from general outdoor supply stores.

Safety Items

PFD (personal flotation device)
Spare paddle
Pump
Dry Bag
Change of warm, dry clothes
Compass
Topo map or NOAA chart (or both)
First-aid kit
Flare
Weather radio
Tide table

Daytrip Items

Drinking water
Suntan lotion
Rain gear
Sunglasses
Trash bag
Flashlight
Paper towels
Camera
Fly rod & reel

Insect repellent
Hat with brim or visor
Long-sleeve shirt
Food
Pocket knife
Waterproof matches
Binoculars
Field guides
Tow Rope

Camping Items

Tent (w/ extra long stakes)
Sleeping bag
Stove
Utensils
Personal hygiene kit
Paddle float

Ground cloth
Sleeping pad
Cook set
Biodegradable soap
Lantern

Backcountry Camping

Many of the trips described in this book are two-day journeys with an overnight spent camping in the wilds. These campsites are often in pristine natural areas that are fragile and very sensitive to human impact. Many were created as preserves to protect valuable natural habitats and the wildlife they support. In other words, people are only visitors. The same guidelines that apply to low-impact wilderness travel elsewhere are valid for kayak camping as well.

In general, you should strive to leave as little trace of your visit behind as possible. This means choosing campsites that will have a minimum impact on sensitive areas; restoring campsites to a natural appearance; packing out all refuse; resisting the impulse to build fire rings; and using a camp stove for cooking, rather than an open fire.

Self-Rescue

The one safety technique that all paddlers should have before getting into a kayak is the ability to perform a wet exit. This is simply a means of exiting the boat in the event of a capsize. Of course, the ability to get back into the kayak doesn't hurt either. If you've never kayaked before, you should practice these skills in a pool or sheltered body of water with a friend on hand to help.

A more advanced self-rescue technique is the Eskimo Roll. Simply put, the Eskimo Roll is a means of righting an overturned kayak without exiting the boat. It is an essential manoeuver in white water kayaking, one that any proficient white water paddler can manage with relative ease. While it is undoubtedly the fastest, easiest way to restore an overturned sea kayak to an upright position, it is not considered an essential skill. The reasons for this are simple. First of all, sea kayaks usually ply much calmer waters than white water kayaks, and instances of capsizing are far fewer. Second, if you do capsize, you won't have thousands of pounds of river current pushing you relentlessly downriver. Unless conditions are particularly severe, you can exit the boat, turn it back upright, pump it out, and get back in. An Eskimo Roll is quicker and easier, but since danger isn't usually a factor, it isn't essential from a rescue point-of-view.

The exception to this rule is during cold weather when the water temperature drops and poses a significant danger. Although the climate in the region covered by this book is generally mild even in winter, days and nights with freezing temperatures do occur. Water temperature drops to just below 50° in January and February. Cold water and winds increase the possibility of hypothermia, the condition that results when the body's core temperature drops substantially below normal. When paddling under such conditions, it is essential that you have a self-rescue strategy at all times. Paddling without one is simply foolish. The benefit of the Eskimo Roll is that it virtually eliminates the time you spend in the water if your kayak capsizes.

In conclusion then, the ability to perform an Eskimo Roll is a useful skill for sea kayaking in the Carolinas, certainly worth learning. During cold weather, it adds a measure of security. But under most conditions, you can get by just fine without it. The truth is, you'll probably take dozens of kayaking trips before you ever end up in the water.

Using this Book

Sea Kayaking the Carolinas is a where-to, as opposed to a how-to, guide to kayaking. While it includes some incidental information about technique and preparation, it was written with the assumption that those using it have received instruction in kayaking from some other source, be it a book, friends, or a course. If you've never kayaked before, please don't use this guide as your sole introduction to the sport. Read other books or magazines on the subject; take a trip with friends who are experienced kayakers; or sign up for a course or guided trip. Outfitters that offer the latter are listed in the back of this book.

The book's layout is intended to help you choose a destination and then get you on the water as quickly and easily as possible. Descriptions of trips are kept short. Rather than describing our own experience in paddling a particular route or area, we have simply provided the necessary amount of information to help you follow the route. We have also attempted to provide the information that is most useful to kayakers planing a trip: location of put-ins and take-outs, on-site sources of information, camping regulations, and the location of water and other facilities.

Each area begins with a descriptive account that provides a general overview. The focus here is on the aspects that make the area an appealing, and often unique, paddling destination. Such things as topography, history, ecology, and current uses are emphasized. The attempt has been to convey a general sense of an area. Following are shorter entries that provide specific information. In order, they are: information, maps, hazards, basecamp, and trip descriptions. What you'll find under each of these headings is described below.

INFORMATION: This section includes the name, address, and phone number of a contact who can supply you with additional information about an area. In most cases, this is the administrative body that oversees the particular area. Often, there is an on-site office or headquarters where you can pick up maps (*not* NOAA charts or USGS topos), brochures, or check on local conditions. This is always a good idea before heading out. We've also included the nearest location of facilities such as water, rest rooms, and pay phones.

MAPS: Along with a compass, a good map should be considered essential equipment for most of the trips described in this book. The best maps for coastal kayaking are the NOAA charts used by almost all boaters and the USGS topographic maps familiar to backpackers and hikers. Which you use is largely a matter of personal preference. The topo maps are best for reading landscapes, while the NOAA charts are particularly good for navigating shallows and tidal flats. For the topos, the 7.5-minute series is preferred because of its large scale. The NOAA charts come in various scales. The 1:40,000 and 1:80,000 charts are the most suitable for kayaking. These are available at most marine supply stores. The USGS topo maps are available at many outdoor supply stores or from the U.S. Geological Survey, Branch of Distribution, Box 25286, DCF, Denver, CO 80255.

The maps included in this book are for illustration purposes only. They are only meant to provide a visual aid to area descriptions and should not be used for navigation.

HAZARDS: This is perhaps the trickiest section in the book. While the large majority of kayaking trips are undertaken without incident, and we don't want to create a misleading sense of apprehension, we also don't want to encourage a false sense of security—or worse, of invulnerability. As with all types of outdoor travel and adventure, an element of risk is always present. Our aim is to help you be aware of that risk so as to minimize it. Under this section we've included only hazards that are particular to an individual area. This does not mean that they are the only hazards that will be encountered. Hazards common to the Carolina coast such as strong winds, rip tides, unpredictable currents, sudden storms, and hurricanes are not included under this section. This does not mean that they should be discounted. In using this section, always treat the list of hazards as incomplete.

BASE CAMP: Unfortunately, we don't all live at the beach. Except for short day-trips close to home, you'll need to find some place to settle down for the night. In keeping with our focus on backcountry travel, we've put the most work into finding primitive campsites or campgrounds that can serve as a convenient base for day-trips or weekend trips into the backcountry. In a few cases there are backcountry campsites designed to accommodate paddlers or primitive backcountry camping is permitted throughout an area, such as at Cape Lookout National Seashore. More often, however, you'll find yourself based at a developed campground near the put-in or take-out. We've also included the town or city with hotels, motels, and B&Bs closest to each area. Just in case you would actually rather sleep in a bed after a day out on the water.

PUT-IN: Directions are given from the nearest large town or highway. Many of the put-ins are developed boat ramps. Others are sandy landings or unimproved ramps designed for canoes and kayaks. All have parking, unless indicated otherwise.

TAKE-OUT: For most trips the take-out and the put-in are the same. While round trips mean that some backtracking is usually necessary, it also means that you don't need to arrive in two cars or arrange a vehicle shuttle. A few of the trips are one way and end at a location different from the put-in.

DAYTRIP: The description of each trip begins with a brief encapsulation that includes trip highlights, beginning and ending points, distance, and a difficulty rating. These last 2 items are described in separate sections below.

At least one daytrip is included for each of the areas in this book. In all but a few cases, the trips range from 5 to 20 miles. Assuming an average paddling speed of 3 mph, this means a trip that ranges in length from just under 2 hours to more than 8. The routes described are suggestions only. For most of the areas, many different route options exist.

TRIP DISTANCE: All distances are given in land miles, rather than nautical miles. The reasons for this is that everybody is familiar with land miles and they are used on the scales of all maps except nautical charts. If you want to convert the distances to nautical miles, simply add 15 percent to the land mile distance. (If you're interested, a nautical mile is 6,076 feet.)

DIFFICULTY RATING: The difficulty rating is a subjective measure devised by the authors of this book to provide readers an easy scale for evaluating trips. The scale runs from 1 to 5, with 1 being the easiest and 5 the most difficult. The numbers of the scale have no meaning outside of this book and do not relate to any other scale. You should also be aware that the scale only refers to conditions encountered on the Carolina coast. In other words, a 5 refers to the most difficult conditions you will encounter paddling the Carolinas, but certainly not the most difficult conditions you could encounter paddling elsewhere.

The criteria used in assigning these ratings are as follows: size of body of water, proximity to dry land or shallow water, strength of current, prevailing wind conditions, ease of rescue, and volume of other boat traffic. In assessing a particular trip, the ratings can be read as follows:

1. Easy, suitable for novices. A good learning environment.
2. Moderately easy, but requiring at least a measure of skill.
3. More difficult. May involve paddling on open water and negotiating hazards. Self-rescue required.
4. Difficult. Involves conditions that require considerable skill.
5. Very difficult. Conditions are as demanding as can be encountered on the Carolina coast. Requires the utmost skill and experience.

These ratings apply to typical paddling conditions during warm weather with water temperatures above 65°. When conditions are less favorable or when the water temperature is below 65°, the difficulty rating would increase depending on the severity of the conditions.

WEEKENDER: The definition of a weekender is two day's paddling with a single overnight. Most of the information for this category is the same as for the daytrip. The major difference is that all weekenders involve some form of camping, usually in a primitive undeveloped area with few or no facilities. In addition to paddling skills, these trips require a knowledge of low-impact backcountry survival. Many of the trips involve making camp on an empty beach or in a wilderness preserve miles from civilization. Overnighting in these remote locales requires additional preparation and care to ensure your own safety and to protect environments that are fragile and sensitive.

North Carolina

North Carolina Key Map

1. Mackay Island NWR
2. Merchants Millpond SP
3. Currituck Banks
4. Historic Edenton
5. Scuppernong River
6. Pettigrew SP
7. Alligator River NWR
8. Bodie Island
9. Hatteras Island
10. Ocracoke Island
11. Mattamuskeet NWR
12. Goose Creek SP
13. Cedar Island NWR
14. North Core Banks
15. South Core Banks
16. Shackleford Banks
17. Bogue Banks
18. Croatan NF
19. Hammocks Beach SP
20. Lake Waccamaw SP
21. Masonboro Island ERR
22. Carolina Beach SP
23. Fort Fisher SRA

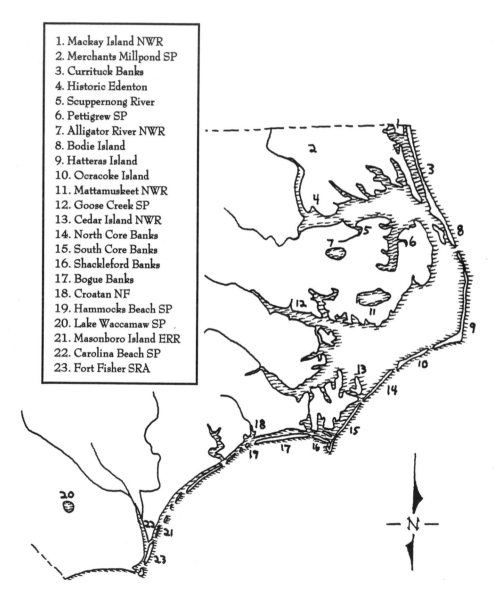

Weather Readings at Beaufort, NC

Month	Air Temp (High)	Water Temp	Wind Speed (mph)	Wind Direction
January	52°	48°	9	NE
February	53°	48°	9	NE
March	58°	54°	10	SSW
April	66°	60°	10	SSW
May	74°	70°	9	SSW
June	80°	75°	8	SSW
July	84°	80°	8	SSW
August	83°	81°	7	SSW
September	79°	80°	8	NNE
October	71°	70°	8	NNE
November	63°	60°	8	NNE
December	55°	54°	8	N

Mackay Island National Wildlife Refuge

North Landing River ◊ Currituck Sound

The Mackay Island NWR was established in 1960 to provide secure habitat along the Atlantic Flyway for migratory waterfowl, especially the greater snow goose. During the fall and winter, thousands of these birds can be seen in the refuge's marshes and impoundments. At one time, a full one-half of the total population of snow geese passed through the refuge annually.

8,000 acres of freshwater marsh, pine-hardwood forest, and agricultural fields are laced by a network of canals and impoundments on Knotts Island. The refuge is the northernmost in North Carolina; in fact, 842 acres lie across the state line in Virginia. In addition to the snow geese, the refuge is used by almost 200 species of birds, ducks, geese, and swans. Common sightings include the majestic great blue heron, great egret, black duck, blue-winged teal, osprey, American kestrel, belted kingfisher, and prothonotary warbler. The bald eagle is sometimes seen as well. A partial list of mammals that inhabit the refuge includes white-tailed deer, gray fox, river otter, mink, nutria, and muskrat. Cottonmouths are also present in significant numbers; paddlers should keep their presence in mind.

This remote corner of Currituck County has a tradition of wildlife conservation that predates the establishment of the refuge. Joseph Knapp, the former owner of the lands that comprise Mackay Island NWR, founded the organization that later became Ducks Unlimited, the largest environmental group whose primary concern is the protection of habitat used by migratory waterfowl. Like other wildlife refuges on this part of the Atlantic coast, Mackay Island was used primarily as hunting grounds when it was in private hands.

With the current wildlife conservation ethic, kayakers have one of the outstanding opportunities in the area to bag ducks and other avian species, but with binoculars or cameras, rather than with rifles. The different waterways of Mackay Island provide a

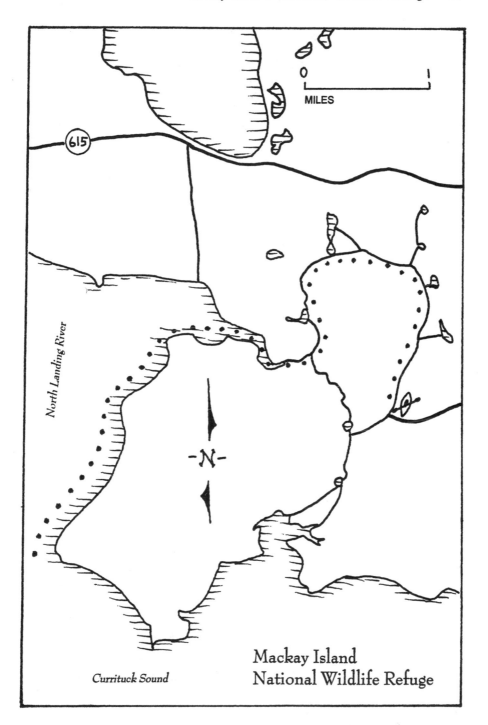

615

MILES

North Landing River

-N-

Currituck Sound

Mackay Island
National Wildlife Refuge

cross section of paddling environments. The sheltered canals that lace the island's marshes provide easy paddling that permits you to concentrate on studying the local flora and fauna. On the other hand, open water surrounds the island on all sides, presenting paddlers with more challenging conditions.

Kayakers need to be aware that the refuge is closed to all boats from October 15 to March 15. This is to preserve the habitat used by migrating waterfowl in as undisturbed a state as possible. At other times of the year, however, you can paddle miles of canals and bays in just about absolute solitude. Since the refuge is only open during daylight hours, multi-day trips must be based off-site.

INFORMATION: Refuge Manager, Mackay Island NWR, P.O. Box 31, Knotts Island, NC 27950-0031; 919/429-3100. A visitor center, where you can pick up photocopied maps of the refuge, bird lists, and other info, is located on the refuge. Restrooms, a pay phone, and water are all inside. The office is open weekdays from 8 AM to 4 PM year round.

MAPS: NOAA chart 11207; USGS Knotts Island, Barco.

HAZARDS: You won't encounter many hazards on the inland waterways of Mackay Island. Fishing boats are a presence on the sounds, but traffic is relatively light.

BASECAMP: Camping is not permitted on the NWR, so if you're coming for more than a day, you have to make other overnight arrangements. A private campground is located on the island. Hotels, motels, and other accommodations can be found in Virginia Beach, VA or Elizabeth City, NC.

PUT-IN: There are 2 put-ins on the refuge. The refuge is reached from road in VA or from a ferry that runs between Knotts Island and Currituck, NC (call 800/BY FERRY for a schedule). The visitor center is on NC-615 1.1 miles S of the NC/VA state line. A boat ramp on Barley's Bay is located about one mile S of the refuge office on NC-615. To get to the other put-in, drive S on NC-615 5.1 miles to a refuge access road. The signed ramp is located at the end of the dirt and gravel road.

TAKE-OUTS: Same as the second put-in above.

DAYTRIP: *The Marshes of Mackay Island. This 12-mile trip makes a circuit of the canals and ponds that break up the refuge's extensive marshes before heading out onto the open water of North Landing River. Difficulty rating: 3.*

From the second put-in above, paddle out along the narrow canal. With the low profile of a kayak, you'll be travelling below the tops of the marsh grasses that cover most of this part of Mackay Island. Intermittent ponds located along the ditches allow for more open vistas. Both habitats offer prime wildlife viewing opportunities. Follow the canals in a counter-clockwise direction until you reach a canal that leads out of the marshes and onto the open expanse of North Landing River. Navigating these narrow waterways requires a good, large-scale map. Paddle S along the refuge's shoreline 3 miles to Live Oak Point. From there, retrace your route back to the boat landing.

Merchants Millpond State Park

Merchants Millpond ◊ Bennett's Creek

Merchants Millpond is one of the most beautiful and haunting natural habitats in coastal North Carolina. It's also one of the most unique and most isolated. Situated in the rural Albemarle region between the Great Dismal Swamp and the Chowan River, the park is a wilderness oasis in the midst of what seems like a sea of surrounding agricultural land. The dominant natural features of the 3,000-acre park are the 760-acre pond the park is named for and a vast cypress swamp located beyond its easterr edge. Although these two habitats are ecologically different, to the visitor they seem barely distinct: the towering tupelo gum trees and majestic bald cypresses hanging tattered flags of Spanish moss spill out of the swamp and into the pond. The result is an aquatic wonderland where each turn of a canoe or kayak opens up unexpected vistas. The aquatic plants that carpet the pond's surface make it seem at times as if you're gliding on a sea of green. Beneath the plants the water has been dyed a deep, dark color by decaying vegetation. The hilly uplands that surround the pond and swamp are covered by a pine/hardwood forest where American beech is the primary species.

The combination of upland and wetland habitats provides sustenance for a broad diversity of wildlife. If you're lucky, you might spot one of the river otters, turtles, water snakes, mink, beaver, or white-tailed deer that inhabit the park. More likely is a sighting of one of almost 200 species of birds that have been counted around Merchants Millpond. These include year-round inhabitants as well as migratory species. Colorful wood ducks and hooded mergansers, graceful great blue herons, showy egrets, and the bright and lively prothonotary warbler are all present in large numbers.

Although flora and fauna thrive in the natural habitats provided by Merchants Millpond, the pond itself isn't a natural

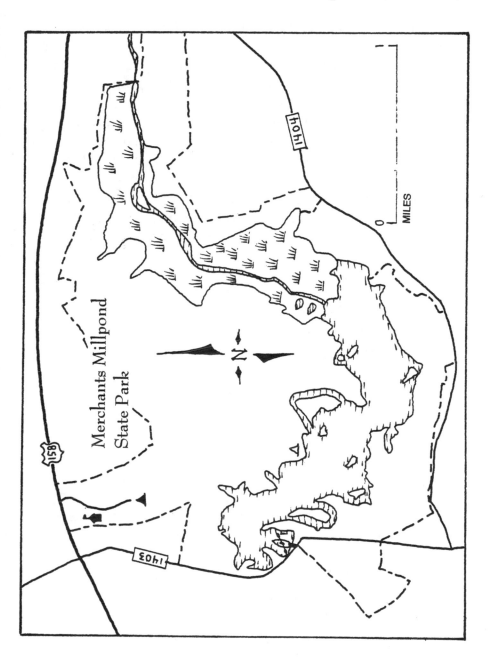

occurrence. It was constructed in 1811, when it was known as Norfleets Millpond. The name change was due to the many merchants who set up shop in the pond's vicinity. Land donations by the owners of the pond and the Nature Conservancy led to the establishment of the park in 1973.

In addition to paddling, park activities include hiking, camping, and fishing. And the dramatic interplay of light and shadow in the swamp and on the millpond gives nature photographers an exceptional canvas to work with. The park is open all year, but the best times to visit are in spring and fall, when the days aren't so hot. Paddlers should be aware that cottonmouths are plentiful in the park, as are ticks during the warm months.

INFORMATION: Merchants Millpond State Park, Route 1, Box 141-A, Gatesville, NC 27938; 919/357-1191. If you're going to camp in the park, be sure to stop by the office first to pick up a permit. Info is available at the office; water, rest rooms, and pay phones are all located in the park.

MAPS: USGS Beckford.

BASE CAMP: With camping facilities that include a car campground and separate hike-in and boat-in camping areas, the park offers plenty of overnight options. Primitive sites cost $5/night, sites in the car campground cost $9/night. If you want to spend more than a day but don't want to camp, the hotels and B&Bs in Elizabeth City are the best bet locally. For listings contact the Elizabeth City Chamber of Commerce (919/335-4365).

PUT-IN: From the junction of US-158 and US-32 E of the park, take US-158 W 5.1 miles to Millpond Rd (SR-1403). Turn L and go 1.4 miles to the parking lot and boat launch, L.

TAKE-OUT: Same as put-in.

DAYTRIP: *Millpond and Swamp Circuit. This unstructured paddle takes in the major habitats that make Merchants Millpond SP such an appealing paddling destination. Difficulty rating: 1.*

Merchants Millpond is the perfect size for a daylong paddle. Not so small that you'll get bored and find yourself repeatedly retracing your route; not so large that you won't get to explore it thoroughly at a leisurely pace. And you'll want to take it slow. Although the word pond conjures images of small bodies of open water, here it refers to an environment where water and forest meet. Although more open than the adjacent swamp, the millpond is dotted with islands, clumps of bald cypress and sweet gum, and solitary trees arching their limbs out over the pond's dark, duckweed-matted surface. The effect of the vegetation is to carve the pond into numerous channels and blind alleys. Even with a couple of dozen paddlers on the water at the same time, it's easy to feel like you're navigating an isolated backwater.

From the put-in beside the main parking area, you can wind your way up and down these channels and circumnavigate the many small islands that dot the pond. When you've explored the pond's environs to your satisfaction, head to Bennett's Creek. This narrow black-water river flows through Lassiter Swamp at the eastern end of the millpond. There you'll find dense stands of bald cypresses draped with the signature Spanish moss and an "enchanted forest" of gum trees bent into otherworldly shapes by mistletoe.

WEEKENDER: *Extended Millpond and Swamp Exploration. This 2-day paddle features an overnight at the backcountry paddling area that can only be reached by boat. Difficulty rating: 1.*

With one of the only paddle-in camping areas at a NC state park, Merchants Millpond is ideal for a weekend kayaking trip. Although the small size of the pond and connecting Bennett's Creek will limit the amount of water you cover, the astonishing natural environment will make you happy to slow your touring pace and linger awhile amidst the gums and bald cypresses that rise from the pond. The same rule that applies to the day-trip holds for an overnight expedition: paddle at your own rate, explore as many of the pond's nooks and crannies as you please, and don't forget to include the tight confines of Bennett's Creek and the magnificent swamp that surrounds it. In short, make the trip your own. The distance from the put-in to the primitive camping area is only about 1 mile, so time isn't really a factor. Take time out for a long picnic lunch, and, if you like, pack hiking boots; the park's network of hiking trails offers a chance to explore the upland forest.

Currituck Banks

Currituck Sound ◊ Atlantic Ocean ◊ North River

Currituck Banks is the end of the line. As you approach from the south on NC-12 (the only road access) you leave the mad commerce of Nags Head and Kill Devil Hills behind. At first the hotels, motels, condos, and beachside attractions give way to tony developments of high-priced homes. Just past Sanderling you enter Currituck County and the development temporarily disappears. Roadside signs request that you exercise caution and watch for any wild ponies that might happen to wander across the road. As you near Corolla another pricey development mushrooms from the dunes, and then you reach the more modest clapboard buildings of Corolla and the Corolla Lighthouse. And then, a little further on, the road ends.

This is the start of Currituck Banks. Although technically the whole long barrier spit that blocks Currituck Sound from the Atlantic Ocean is Currituck Banks, here the designation applies only to the undeveloped 11-mile stretch between Corolla and the Virginia state line. There's not much along that stretch except for the natural habitats endemic to barrier islands: beach, dune, shrub thicket, maritime forest, saltwater marsh, and tidal flat. You might stumble across a few relict fishermen or decoy carvers, but that's about it.

The unspoiled beauty of this part of the North Carolina coast is likely to remain that way, at least for a while longer. The reason is that a large portion of the land between Corolla and Virginia is publicly owned. Although the 2,800-acre preserve site is divided up among the Currituck National Wildlife Refuge, the Currituck Banks Estuarine Research Reserve, and the Nature Conservancy, the three groups manage the land cooperatively to meet the dual aims of conservation and field study. Toward that purpose, the land has been left entirely undeveloped. There's no visitor center or other amenities, and the only way to get there is by boat, on

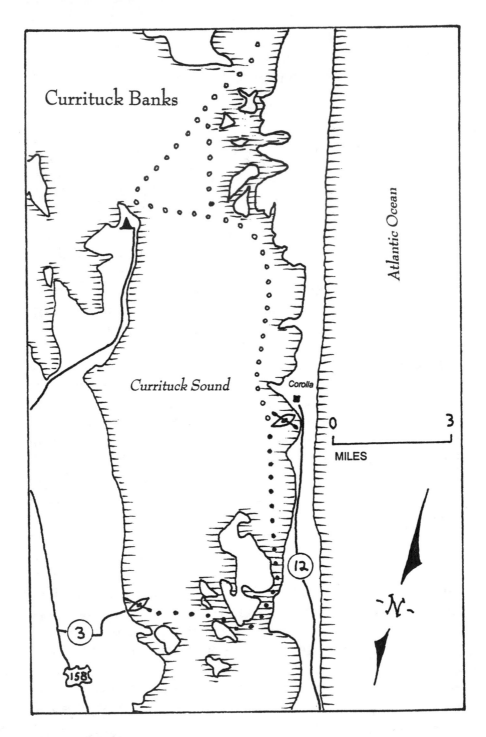

Currituck Banks

Currituck Sound

Atlantic Ocean

Corolla

foot, or on the beach via 4WD vehicle.

Like all barrier land masses, Currituck Banks is a classic merger of land and water. On the ocean side the Atlantic surf crashes into mile after mile of wide sand beach. On the sound side the meeting is softer and more subtle. The freshwater and brackish marshes and tidal flats that line the back of the banks are neither entirely water or land. And unlike the water in most of North Carolina's sounds, Currituck Sound consists almost entirely of freshwater, a result of the lack of an ocean inlet nearby. On the marshes, vast clusters of giant cordgrass, black needlerush, and cattails dominate. In the tidal flats—tides in Currituck Sound are caused by changing wind direction, not by lunar cycles—a soft bottom of mud and sand appears and disappears with the changing water levels.

Prior the 1823, Currituck Sound had been connected to the Atlantic Ocean by at least one inlet, sometimes by as many as three. Currituck Inlet originally marked the North Carolina–Virginia state line. Today the nearest inlet is Oregon Inlet, 45 miles to the south. The closure of the last inlet began a process of change in Currituck Sound that has resulted in its current profile. The water gradually changed over from saltwater to freshwater, or more accurately, brackish, since slight traces of salt still remain. With the different water came different lifeforms. Currently the marshes and shallow waters of the sound are popular resting places with ducks, geese, and swans making their annual migrations along the Atlantic Flyway. And the fish beneath the surface are those most often associated with North Carolina's rivers and lakes: largemouth bass, chain pickerel, black crappie, channel catfish, and yellow perch. On the ocean side, of course, the array of saltwater fish common to the Carolina coast can be caught in the surf.

The waters of Currituck Sound are shallow, averaging about 5 feet deep, with maximum depths of just over 10 feet. Paddlers will find a kayak is an ideal vessel for exploring the intriguing estuary habitats of Currituck Sound. The Intracoastal Waterway passes to the west of the area, reducing boat traffic. Most other boats on the water will belong to fishermen, but their numbers aren't usually so great as to disrupt a cross-sound paddle. While the preserve is limited to a relatively small stretch of barrier spit north of Corolla, kayakers will find plenty to explore along the entire length of Currituck Banks. And while access in the nature preserves is rather difficult, boat ramps in Duck, Corolla, and on the mainland side of the sound offer paddlers plenty of put-in and take-out options. Of course, if you want to paddle the ocean side of the banks, you'll have to tote your kayak across the beach—unless you have a 4WD vehicle and can drive out onto the beach. Whether you want to paddle the sound or the ocean, you'll have to commit to one or the other—getting from sound to sea or vice-versa requires a 90-mile paddle or a difficult portage through fragile habitats.

INFORMATION: Refuge Manager, Currituck National Wildlife Refuge, P.O. Box 39, Knott's Island, NC 27950; 919/429-3100 or Currituck Banks Estuarine Research Reserve, Division of Coastal Management, P.O. Box 27687, Raleigh, NC 27611-7687; 919/733-2293. There's no information center or facilities of any kind on the public portion of Currituck Banks. Water, rest rooms, and other amenities are available in Corolla and Duck on the barrier spit, and at several small towns on the mainland.

MAPS: NOAA chart 12205; USGS Corolla, Barco, Massey Islands, Coinjock.

HAZARDS: Fishing and pleasure boats ply these waters with some frequency. Although lunar tides are not a concern, the sound's open waters can get pretty rough when the wind is up.

BASE CAMP: Camping is not permitted on any of the public land on Currituck Banks. Campgrounds are scarce on the banks too, with the closest ones in Kill Devil Hills. A private campground located at Goose Point on the mainland side of Currituck Sound is ideally located for trips on the sound. A few hotels and motels can be found around Duck, with dozens more down toward Nags Head. Contact the Currituck County Manager (919/232-2075) for info.

PUT-IN: Boat ramps are located on the mainland side of the sound and on Currituck Banks. On the mainland, use Poplar Branch Landing: from the junction of US-158 and NC-12 in Kitty Hawk, take US-158 N 20 miles to NC-3. Turn R and go 2.2 miles to the end of the road and boat ramp.

On Currituck Banks, there's a boat ramp next to the huge water tower on NC-12 in the town of Duck. Another ramp is located in Corolla at the historic Whalehead Club (publicly owned now and the future site of the Currituck Wildlife Museum) 0.1 miles S of the Currituck Lighthouse on NC-12.

TAKE-OUT: Same as the put-ins above.

DAYTRIP: *Currituck Sound Exploration. A 19-mile loop paddle that crosses the sound and follows the shoreline of Currituck Banks. Highlights are estuarine habitats, excellent opportunities for bird watching, and the historic lighthouse in Corolla. Difficulty rating: 3.*

From the Poplar Branch Landing put-in, paddle E across Currituck Sound. Unlike other parts of the sound, shelter is provided here by a series of marsh islands that grow out of the shallow waters all the way from mainland to barrier spit. Continue due E through Lone Oak Channel until you reach the marsh at the back of Currituck Banks, a total distance of 3.5 miles from the put-in. Turn N and paddle 2 miles through a narrow channel to Sanders Bay. Continue N, following the shoreline to the village of Corolla and the Currituck Lighthouse. Take advantage of the red-brick lighthouse as a navigational aid. After 4 miles you'll reach Whale Head Bay and the lighthouse. You can tie up at a long dock that extends into the sound here. Get out and have a look at the Historic lighthouse or have a picnic lunch. When you're ready to return, turn around and retrace your route back to the put-in.

If you'd prefer to start and end your paddle on Currituck Banks instead of the mainland, you can simply reverse the order of this trip by using the boat ramp at the old Whalehead Club as the put-in/take-out.

WEEKENDER: *Currituck Banks, Currituck Sound. A 35-mile one-way paddle that follows both shores of Currituck Sound and passes by the eastern side of Knotts Island. This trip requires 2 cars or a vehicle shuttle. Difficulty rating: 3.*

Put in at the boat ramp at Poplar Branch Landing on the mainland. Currituck Sound here is about 4 miles across, with large islands of brackish marsh across the whole distance. These are separated by numerous small channels and bays, excellent places to explore in a kayak and good sites for birdwatching. Begin the trip by manoeuvering through these islands as you cross the sound. When you reach Currituck Banks, turn N and follow the shoreline, using the Currituck Lighthouse as a landmark. It's a 6-mile paddle to the lighthouse and the village of Corolla. Continue N, paddling between the shoreline and Mary Island. Ships Bay and Jenkins Cove are a couple of natural anchorages on the Currituck NWR. 2.5 miles past the lighthouse reach Monkey Island. Turn W and cross the sound to the Hampton Lodge Campground (open seasonally; 919/453-2732) at Goose Point.

On day 2, begin by crossing the sound again in an ENE direction. At 2 miles you'll reach another series of large marshy islands. Turn N and either skirt them to the W or choose a channel and paddle through them. After 3.5 miles you leave the islands behind and enter Knotts Island Bay, with Knotts Island on the L. You can paddle 5 miles N to the Virginia State Line and Back Bay, or take a slower pace and poke around the marshes, channels, and shoreline of Knotts Island. When you're ready to return to the put-in, retrace your route back S along the coast of Currituck Banks and take out in Corolla at the Whalehead Club boat ramp.

Historic Edenton

Albemarle Sound ◊ Pembroke Creek ◊ Queen Anne's Creek

Coastal North Carolina features mile after mile of pristine natural environments that for reasons of geography, weather, and economics have been spared development over the years. On the other hand, it also features towns and cities whose importance dates back to the earliest days of colonial America and the United States. A few of these have been preserved with large segments of their historic heritage intact. Historic Edenton exemplifies this latter category.

Established on the northern shore of Albemarle Sound in the seventeenth century, by the beginning of the eighteenth it was the second-largest port in the colonies and a major intellectual and cultural center. It was home to Joseph Hewes, a signer of the Declaration of Independence and one of the leading statesmen of the fledgling nation. A monument to him stands at the foot of the courthouse. The city was also at the center of a sectional dispute at a time in North Carolina history when north versus south referred to the rivalry between the Albemarle and lower Cape Fear Regions in governing the colony.

The town grew up around the port at the head of Edenton Bay, and the waterfront remains the center of the exceedingly attractive downtown area. Listed on the National Register of Historic Places, the blocks that extend to water's edge are a combination of green spaces and many of the small city's oldest and most significant buildings. Included among these are the Chowan County Courthouse (1767), the Cupola House (c. 1758), and the Barker House (1782). All of these can be seen from the water. Others can be inspected by following the route of the Historic Edenton Walking Tour, a National Recreation Trail well worth the hour it takes to complete.

For kayakers, the waterfront area is doubly enjoyable, since it can be experienced from the water or land. A small dock has been

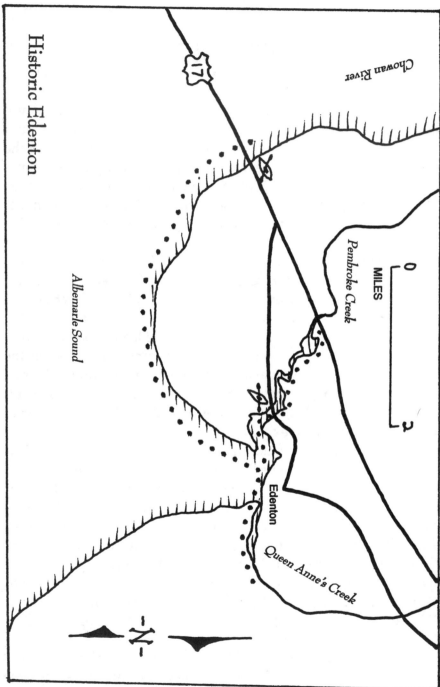

Historic Edenton

Chowan River

Pembroke Creek

Albemarle Sound

Edenton

Queen Anne's Creek

MILES

0

2

built in a waterfront park to make it easy to land and wander through the downtown and waterfront area.

Just minutes away from the historic downtown district, you can paddle through the midst of unspoiled natural habitats. Pembroke Creek and Queen Anne's Creek flow into Edenton Bay from opposite ends. Both are small, attractive waterways that flow through swamp forests where the bald cypresses grow out into the water and flutter loose strands of Spanish moss. These creeks are easily explored by kayak, and except for maybe a small handful of fishermen, you should have the place to yourself. Or, if you'd prefer the challenge of open water, paddle out onto Albemarle Sound or up the vast Chowan River. In fact, Edenton Bay is a fairly open anchorage on the sound, with conditions that can get pretty choppy when the wind is up.

INFORMATION: Historic Edenton, P.O. Box 474, Edenton, NC 27932; 919/482-2637. The visitor center is located downtown at 108 N Broad St. You can pick up information inside, including a map and guide to the Historic Edenton Walking Tour. A 14-minute film on the town's history can also be viewed.

MAPS: NOAA chart 12205; USGS Edenton, Edenhouse.

HAZARDS: The bridge across the Chowan River doesn't offer much clearance between trestles. When the water's rough, getting through can be a little tricky.

BASE CAMP: Although there's no public campground in town, there is a private one: the Sandy Point Campground, located on NC-32 just N of the Albemarle Sound Bridge. It's open from May 15 to Labor Day. Edenton is also home to numerous B&Bs, hotels, and motels. For more info, contact Historic Edenton at the phone number and address above.

PUT-INS: For daytrip 1, put-in at the Pembroke Fishing Center. From the junction of W Queen St and S Broad St in downtown Edenton, take W Queen St W 1.3 miles to the boat ramp on the R.

A $2 launch fee is charged.

For daytrip 2, put in on the Chowan River. Drive 2.1 miles W past the Pembroke Fishing Center on W. Queen St to US-17. Turn L and go 0.9 miles to the boat ramp on the R just before the bridge across the Chowan River. There's also a put-in/take-out on the downtown docks. It's located just behind the ancient tug anchored at the waterfront—you can't miss it.

TAKE-OUTS: Same as the put-in for each trip.

DAYTRIP 1: *The Historic Edenton Waterfront. A 10-mile paddle that takes in the natural habitats on the town's perimeter and the historic downtown area. Difficulty rating: 2.*

From the put-in on Pembroke Creek, paddle upstream between the dense swamp forest that grows on both banks. The creek narrows considerably after the bridge across US-17 as you make your way toward its headwaters. After about 3 miles, turn around and paddle back past the put-in to the creek's mouth on Edenton Bay. Here the city's waterfront comes into view and conditions on the water change. From the sheltered creek you enter the open water of Albemarle Sound. Paddle less than a quarter-mile to the boat dock behind the tug. Don't pass up the chance to get out and explore this part of the city on foot. You can take in most of the sights by walking less than a mile, and it really is one of the most attractive towns on the entire Atlantic coast. Have lunch at one of the downtown eateries or pack your own and eat in one of the waterfront parks.

When you're ready to resume paddling, continue across Edenton Bay to the mouth of Queen Anne's Creek. Paddle under the wooden bridge and head upstream. You can paddle about 2 miles before the creek becomes too narrow a passageway. When you reach that point, turn around and retrace your route to the put-in on Pembroke Creek.

DAYTRIP 2: *Chowan River to Edenton Bay. A 12-mile round trip on the Chowan River and Albemarle Sound. Highlights are the swamp forest along the shore and Historic Edenton. Difficulty rating: 3.*

Put in at the WRC boat ramp on the Chowan River. Paddle back under the bridge, exercising caution as you squeeze between the wood trestles. Follow the shoreline as it curves around to Edenton Bay and the mouths of Pembroke Creek and Queen Anne Creek. The total distance is about 6 miles. There are good opportunities for viewing wildlife, particularly waterfowl and wading birds, along the route. When you reach the town docks, tie up at the floating dock beside the tug and spend some time wandering downtown. After some lunch or time spent viewing Edenton's historic attractions, paddle back along the same route to the put-in. If you'd rather extend your trip a little, paddle up either Queen Anne's Creek or Pembroke Creek for a mile or two.

Scuppernong River

Scuppernong River ◊ Albemarle Sound

In a region defined by waterways both large and small, the Scuppernong stands out as one of the most enchanting. Rising in one of the few remaining tracts of dense swamp forest that once blanketed the entire Albemarle region, the blackwater creek meanders along a twisting course for some 20 miles before emptying into Albemarle Sound. Along its route it flows not far from Lake Phelps and the historic Somerset Place Plantation and the historic town of Columbia, the county seat of Tyrell County. Several of the ditches that were dug to drain the swamp connect the river to the lake, though obstructions are abundant and currently the route can't be paddled without difficulty. Plans are under way, however, to open up a canoe/kayak trail that will run from Columbia all the way to Lake Phelps.

The region's history begins with the native Americans who once inhabited the area. Artifacts excavated from the area around Lake Phelps indicate that the area has been populated for more than 10,000 years. European presence began in the eighteenth century, when the vast impenetrable wilderness was known as the Great Eastern Dismal. By the end of that century Somerset Place Plantation was in full swing between the Scuppernong River and Lake Phelps. The rice, corn, and wheat plantation encompassed more than 100,000 acres and relied on the labor of more than 300 slaves. It was these slaves who built the system of canals that still connect the river to the lake.

While most of the vast swamp that fired the imaginations of early visitors was cleared to create productive agricultural land, the Scuppernong River flows through a narrow corridor of cypress-gum swamp forest. Here are the towering trees and wild grape vines—some as much as a foot in diameter—that enthralled and unsettled the region's first settlers. The cypresses served a utilitarian purpose even before they were logged for timber: the

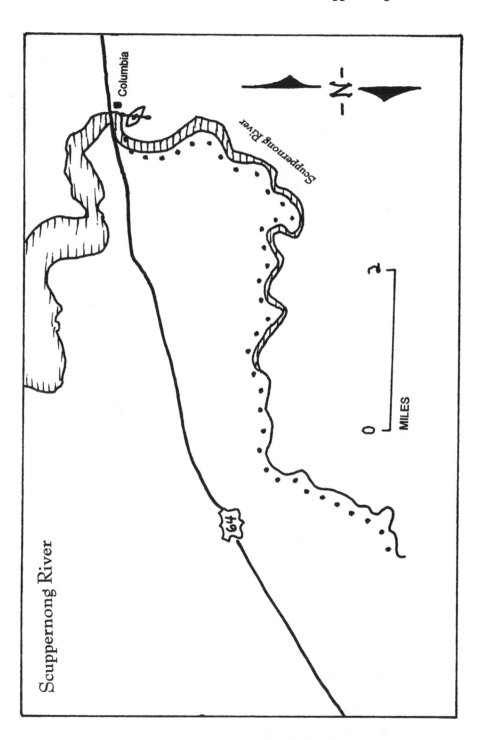

Scuppernong River

Algonquin tribe used them to construct their dugout canoes as early as 2,000 B.C.

The Scuppernong River presents paddlers with three relatively distinct sections. Near its headwaters southwest of Creswell, the river is a narrow creek that moves beneath the overhanging limbs and vegetation of the swamp that spreads out from either bank. As it nears the historic town of Columbia it widens somewhat—to perhaps a couple hundred feet across. Here is the main river access and a chance to get off the river and stroll through the waterfront district of the pleasant, laid-back town. Once the river passes Columbia it widens still more, until its open waters begin to resemble more closely the vast sound into which it empties.

The Scuppernong offers kayakers a rare chance to travel back in time, through a river corridor that recalls the primeval past of an unsettled continent not yet altered by the work of humans.

INFORMATION: Tyrell County Visitor Center, 203 Ludington Dr., Columbia, NC 27925; 919/796-1000. The visitor center is located just off US-64 on the Columbia Waterfront. Water, restrooms, and a pay phone are all located there. In summer, you can rent kayaks out back not more than 20 feet from the river's edge.

MAPS: USGS Columbia West, Creswell Southeast, Creswell.

BASE CAMP: Although there are no camping facilities on the Scuppernong River, the campground at Pettigrew State Park is just a short drive west. For a bed to sleep in, there's a B&B in the town of Columbia. Other nearby accommodations are available in Manteo or Plymouth.

PUT-IN: Park in the visitor center on US-64 in downtown Columbia. There's a boat ramp behind the visitor center on the E shore of the river.

TAKE-OUT: Same as the put-in.

DAYTRIP: *Scuppernong River Exploration. A 10–20-mile trip into the heart of the swamp forest that engulfs the river. The main attraction is the chance to experience the wetland habitat that once covered most of this part of the state. Difficulty rating: 2.*

Put in behind the visitor center. Follow the river upstream from the town of Columbia. As the river gradually narrows, the swamp forest that crowds both banks looms closer and closer. This offers an excellent opportunity to observe the flora and fauna of an amazingly diverse natural habitat up close. Many of the species of birds and plants are exotic and intriguing. Others, such as the cottonmouth and mosquitoes, are less welcome, but none the less important to the functioning of the wetland ecosystem. You can paddle the river one-way for about 16 miles to the town of Cherry. Unless you're in a marathoning mood, you'll want to turn back well before that and paddle back downstream to the take-out at the visitor center. An alternative is to plan a one-way trip with a take-out at one of the bridges that cross the river's upper reaches.

Alligator River National Wildlife Refuge

Milltail Creek ◊ Alligator River ◊ Albemarle Sound

When the federal government was looking for a coastal site for the reintroduction of the endangered red wolf, they needed an area large enough to accommodate the wolves' peripatetic habits and remote enough to minimize contact with civilization. They settled on the Alligator River NWR. The refuge sprawls across 150,000 acres of low-lying coastal habitat on a broad peninsula between the eponymous river and Croatan Sound. Not much more than a stone's throw from the location of the first English settlement in the New World, the refuge is a wild region where water and earth meet and mingle. It's also one of the largest tracts of wilderness on the Atlantic coast.

For kayakers the open waters of the river and sounds that surround the refuge, as well as the more intimate creeks, bays, and lakes that drain its pervasive swamp forest, are a watery paradise. Most paddlers forego the less interesting (and more commercially busy) open waters in favor of the black, stillwater creeks and cuts at the heart of the refuge. Adding to the attraction are the first marked canoe and kayak trails on a national wildlife refuge in North Carolina. The trails cover 13 miles of water, and though they have increased traffic (a relative term in this remote backcountry) on the refuge's waterways, they also provide one of the best means for exploring the amazingly rich, and increasingly rare, wetland habitat that the Alligator River NWR was created to protect.

That habitat includes brackish marshes, pine and hardwood forests, cypress hardwood swamp, cranberry bogs, and relict agricultural fields. The wetlands that still remain on refuge lands are just a small percentage of those that once extended from end to end of the low-lying peninsula and earned the region the moniker Great Alligator Swamp. Major draining projects diverted much of the water so that the land could be used for productive

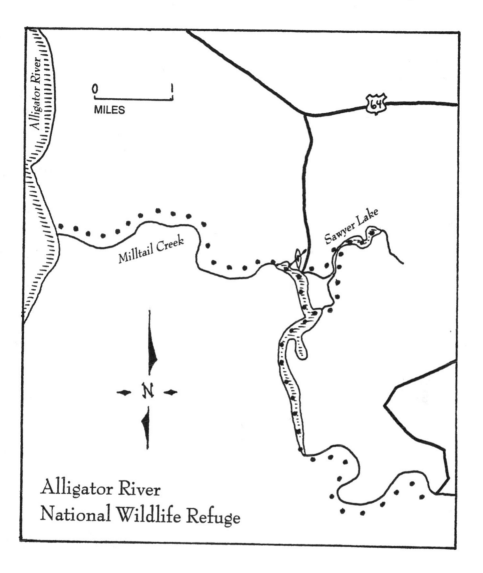

MILES

Alligator River

Milltail Creek

Sawyer Lake

N

Alligator River
National Wildlife Refuge

farmland. One of the refuge's ongoing missions is to restore as much of the wetland habitat as possible. This includes the extensive areas once covered by Atlantic white cedars. Currently only a few isolated pockets of these important trees remain. Wetlands are vital ecosystems because of the number and diversity of wildlife species they support. Among large mammals at Alligator River NWR are the black bear, white-tailed deer, and the recently reintroduced red wolf. Other endangered species that inhabit the refuge are the bald eagle, peregrine falcon, American alligator, and red-cockaded woodpecker.

While paddlers will be extremely lucky to spy a member of one of the endangered or threatened species, much of the reserve's fauna is abundant and commonly seen. Odds are good that as you paddle the narrow corridors through the swamp you'll flush at least one great blue heron, spot a turtle sunning itself on a dead log, or hear the rat-a-tat of the pileated woodpecker. One refuge inhabitant you'll want to avoid is the cottonmouth. Keep a lookout for these poisonous snakes, especially during warm weather.

The refuge is open all year during daylight hours only. Camping is not allowed, so daytrip paddles only are possible. For multi-day explorations of the area, camp at the NPS campground on Bodie Island (part of Cape Hatteras NS). Freshwater fishing, hiking, and mountain biking are other possible outdoor activities on the refuge.

INFORMATION: Alligator River NWR, P.O. Box 1969, Manteo, NC 27954; 919/473-1131. On-site information is limited to a kiosk at the jct of Milltail Creek Rd and US-64. Plans are in the works to build a visitor center.

MAPS: USGS Buffalo City.

HAZARDS: Although the canoe/kayak trails pass through remote wilderness, the refuge is also used by fishermen in motor boats and, in winter and fall, by hunters. The black bears and red wolves that inhabit the refuge, shy of humans, are all but harmless unless provoked. The narrow ditches can become obstructed with downed trees or hanging vegetation.

BASE CAMP: Camping is not allowed on the refuge. There are hotels, B&Bs, and campgrounds in Manteo on Roanoke Island, less than a half-hour drive west. The nearest public campground is Oregon Inlet on Bodie Island.

PUT-IN: From the jct of US-64 and US-264 near Manns Harbor, take US-64 W 7.7 mi (4 mi E of the Lindsay C. Warren bridge across the Alligator River) to Buffalo City Rd. Turn L onto the dirt and gravel road and go 2 mi to a small parking area and boat launch.

TAKE-OUT: Same as above for both trips.

DAYTRIP 1: *In the Heart of the Swamp. This 11-mile round-trip paddle begins on the open water of Boat Bay before following lazy, blackwater Milltail Creek upstream through dense swamp and bottomland forest. The route is blazed with blue bands. Difficulty rating: 1.*

From the Buffalo City Rd put-in, paddle out onto Boat Bay and follow it south. The Bay is a natural bulge in narrow Milltail Creek. Although you'll probably see some anglers as you navigate the bay's open waters, most of what you'll see is swamp forest and sky. Except for the occasional flyby of a military jet on a training run (an unfortunate occurrence), the silence is total. Follow the bay S 3 miles to where it narrows again into Milltail Creek. The channel is narrow—not more than 50 feet across—and the sense of paddling deep into remote wilderness is strong. Follow the creek 2.5 miles to a bridge and another access on dirt Milltail Rd. Return along the same route to the put-in.

DAYTRIP 2: *Sawyer Lake/Milltail Creek Combo. This 13-mile tour follows 3 connecting trails on 5 different bodies of water. The habitats include a lake, bay, and stillwater creek, with dense swamp forest on all sides. Difficulty rating: 2.*

From the put-in, follow the red and green blazes through a very narrow canal to Sawyer Lake. Obstructions are a possibility, though the water trail is maintained. When you exit the canal on the lake, follow the green bands to its end and return along the opposite shore. After 4 miles rejoin the red trail and paddle through a narrow cut less than a quarter mile to Boat Bay. When you reach the open waters of the bay, turn R and follow the shoreline past the put-in to lower Milltail Creek. Here is the start of the yellow trail, which leads to the Alligator River. Enter the creek and paddle 4 miles along its narrow, twisting course. The marshlands on either side are prime wildlife-viewing locations. When you reach the mouth at the Alligator River either enter the river or return along the same route to the put-in. Keep in mind that conditions on the vast river are quite different from the sheltered, flatwater creek. Almost 5 miles across, the Alligator River is open water, with strong winds and choppy water not at all unusual.

Pettigrew State Park
Lake Phelps

Pettigrew State Park sits on the shore of one of those intriguing anomalies of the North Carolina coastal plain, the Carolina bay lake. The term Carolina bay doesn't refer to the bodies of water, but to the vegetation common to them: red bay, loblolly bay, and sweet bay. In all, some 500,000 Carolina bays dot the coastal plain between New Jersey and Georgia. Only a handful—all in North Carolina—still hold water, and these seem to be gradually shrinking. With rainfall as their only source of water, most have long dried out and been overrun with vegetation, though the elliptical depressions still remain. Scientists aren't sure how they first got there—theories include underwater springs, meteor showers, and wind and wave action—but all share similar features. These include an oval shape, shallow water not usually more than 10 feet deep, a sand and peat bottom, and a sandy shoreline at the southeastern end. Dense shrub thickets known as *pocosins*—an Algonquin word that means swamp on a hill—are usually found around their edge.

Five miles across and covering 16,600 acres of water, Lake Phelps is a natural destination for paddlers. The first paddlers to ply the lake's clear waters were the Algonquin Indians. Archaeologists have unearthed 30 dugout canoes from the lake bed, some dating back more than 4,000 years. These vessels aren't just of local interest: only one other canoe in the United States has been found older than some of those from Lake Phelps, and one 37-footer is the longest that's been found in the Southeast. The raw material the Algonquian tribe used for their canoes can still be seen all around the lake—bald cypress trees. Other artifacts found around the lake put the tribe's presence here as early as 8,000 B.C.

The lake was probably a popular locale of the Algonquin tribe for some of the same reasons it draws visitors today. The crystal-clear waters are home to large populations of several game fish,

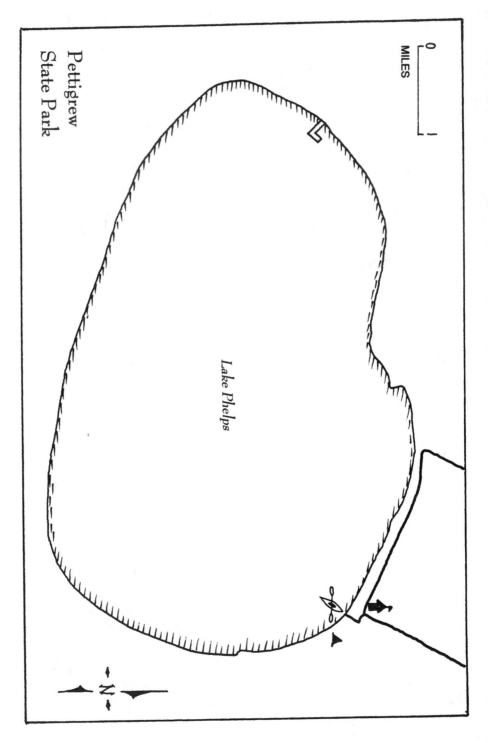

including largemouth bass and yellow perch. And the lake is an important natural habitat that provides sustenance for many different species of wildlife. In winter the lake's surface becomes crowded with migrating swans, geese, and ducks. Great blue herons, osprey, belted kingfishers, and egrets are some of the other bird species you might see. Mammals that frequent the area around the lake include white-tailed deer, black bear, river otter, bobcat, and mink. The lake is rimmed by forest hardwoods that include an unusual number of state champions, and even one national champion. Bald cypress is the most abundant species, and the one most characteristic of the southern bottomland swamp forest that used to cover this part of the state. Spanish moss hangs in loose tatters at water's edge, creating the moodiness so often associated with southern wetlands.

For kayakers, the lake offers a chance to explore the intriguing habitat of a Carolina bay lake up close. It also offers conditions that will appeal to paddlers of any skill level. Although conditions can get rough when the wind is up, most days the surface of the lake shows barely a ripple.

INFORMATION: Superintendent, Pettigrew State Park, Route 1, Box 336, Creswell, NC 27928; 919/797-4475. Information available in the park includes a map of the lake and a brochure describing the area's natural and human history. Water and restrooms are both located near the boat ramp.

MAPS: USGS Creswell, Roper South, New Lake NW.

HAZARDS: Wind can whip the often placid surface of Lake Phelps into a choppy froth. Anglers fishing from motor boats are a presence on the lake, but their numbers usually aren't too large.

BASE CAMP: Pettigrew SP is home to a pleasant small campground just a stone's throw from the water's edge. 13 large sites are spread out at the edge of a dense, lush band of forest that rims the lake. Some of the champion trees are in the area. Sites cost $9/night. The boat access is only a short walk away.

PUT-IN: From US-64 in Creswell, turn S onto Sixth St. Go 0.3 miles and turn L onto Main St. Drive 1.8 miles to Thirty Foot Canal Rd (SR-1160). Turn R and go 5.6 miles to Lakeshore Dr (SR-1166). Turn L and then immediately R into the state park. The boat ramp is straight ahead.

TAKE-OUT: Same as the put-in.

DAYTRIP: *Lake Phelps Circuit. A 20-mile paddle around the lake's perimeter, beginning and ending at the state park boat ramp. Difficulty rating: 2.*

The daytrip follows the lakeshore all the way around the lake's perimeter. While a quick glance at Lake Phelps can leave one with the impression that it's a dull bowl of water with no intriguing inlets, coves, or arms to explore, closer inspection reveals a different world. For one thing, you can see the lake bottom almost anywhere on the lake where lily pads don't obscure the view. This means the chance to observe fish and other aquatic wildlife without the use of snorkeling or scuba equipment. And if you keep close to the shoreline, you can marvel at the size and variety of the tree species. You'll get to observe more huge trees of different species than at any other single location on the coastal plain. The small dock at the lake's western edge—about halfway around the lake from the put-in—makes a nice stopover place for lunch. And the temptation to bring a fly rod and wade the shallow waters may be too much to resist.

WEEKENDER: *Extended Lake Phelps Paddle. A 2-day exploration of the lake's natural habitats, with an overnight in the park campground. Difficulty rating: 1.*

Although Lake Phelps is just about the right size for a vigorous day's paddle, the presence of a really nice campground right at its edge might tempt you to stay an extra day. If that's the case, then slow down the speed of your exploration and stretch it into 2 days. You can even put the kayak away for half a day and hike the park's trails or examine some of the historical artifacts at Somerset Place next door. Exhibits reveal what life was like on a plantation in the ante-bellum South. Or dock at the new pier at the lake's western end. It's part of the Pocosin Lake NWR. You can picnic here, drop a line in the water, or hike some of the gated dirt roads that criss-cross the refuge. You might even flush some game. If you hike the refuge in fall or winter, however, wear blaze orange and keep an eye out for hunters

Cape Hatteras National Seashore

Croatan Sound ◊ Roanoke Sound ◊ Pamlico Sound ◊ Atlantic Ocean

In many ways, Cape Hatteras is synonymous with the Outer Banks. The words conjure images that reflect the most appealing and the most notorious elements of the North Carolina coast. The appeal stems from the seemingly endless miles of pristine beaches, some of the best sport fishing on the East Coast, minimal development, and a lighthouse that may be the most photographed landmark in the entire state. The dangers of Cape Hatteras are no less reputed. The treacherous waters just off the coast have seen the destruction of so many ships and their crews that the area has more than earned the sobriquet "graveyard of the Atlantic." And when a hurricane lashes into the North Carolina coast, Cape Hatteras often bears the worst the storm has to offer. The deadly currents, shifting shoals, and extreme weather are all the result of geography: Cape Hatteras is at the outermost extent of the long string of barrier islands that line this part of the Atlantic coast. The bent elbow of the cape is cut off from the mainland by the expansive waters of Pamlico Sound, and it sits right at the point where opposing Atlantic currents crash together.

But Cape Hatteras has its benign side as well. And it's this that draws visitors from all over the eastern United States and beyond. The national seashore is a mecca for anglers, swimmers, wind-surfers, sunbathers, naturalists, bird-watchers, surfers, and of course sea kayakers. Like Cape Lookout to the south, the profile of Cape Hatteras is long and narrow. Three islands—from north to south Bodie, Hatteras, and Ocracoke—span 80 miles, with a width that averages from one to three miles. Although a single ribbon of asphalt runs the length of the islands (A free ferry connects Ocracoke and Hatteras) and a handful of small communities offer amenities such as hotels and restaurants, for the most part, the islands remain wonderfully undeveloped.

This leaves the paddler or other visitor with the opportunity to explore the amazingly dynamic ecology and geography of barrier islands. The primary habitats that comprise the barrier island system are oceanfront beach, dunes, sand flats with shrub thickets, maritime forest, salt and brackish marsh, and tidal flats. A few fresh-water impoundments are also found on the islands, particularly at Pea Island National Wildlife Refuge, where they play a role in wildlife conservation. Behind the islands is Pamlico Sound, the second largest body of inland water (Chesapeake Bay is largest) on the East Coast. Although the waters of the sound average only 10 to 20 feet deep, high winds can whip up waves that rival those of any sea.

The combination of ocean, sound, and barrier island is naturally alluring to just about every species of bird that inhabits the coastal plain. More than 400 species have been observed on the Outer Banks. While this dazzling variety draws bird watchers from all points of the compass, almost as popular with visitors is the herd of wild horses that roams Ocracoke Island. Other large mammals on the islands are scarce due to the inhospitable climate.

For kayakers, Cape Hatteras NS offers some of the best paddling opportunities in the state. And unlike Cape Lookout to the south, access is made easy by the highway that runs the length of the seashore and the developed campgrounds on the islands. The easy access isn't without tradeoffs, of course. First, you won't have the opportunity to explore a truly primitive barrier island ecosystem, though Cape Hatteras offers a pretty close approximation. Second, you'll have to share the islands with hundreds, if not thousands, of other visitors. And third, since camping outside of developed campgrounds isn't permitted, there's no opportunity for multi-day expeditions where you camp on the beach or in the sand flats. For day trips and even multi-day trips from a base camp, however, the islands of Cape Hatteras really can't be beat.

Planning a trip takes less work than in more remote regions, since the amenities of civilization are never very far away. Water is easily had on the islands, and if you run low on food or other supplies, a quick stop at a convenience store or other shop will remedy the situation. And if you want to explore different parts of the national seashore on short trips, easy road access makes it possible. In short, Cape Hatteras offers paddlers an appealing compromise between unsullied wilderness and the comforts of civilization.

INFORMATION: Superintendent, Cape Hatteras National Seashore, Route 1, Box 675, Manteo, NC 27954; 919/473-2111. When you visit the NS, you can pick up maps, brochures, and other info at any of 4 visitor centers. Whalebone Junction is located on Bodie Island just S of the jct of US-64 and NC-12. Other visitor centers are located at the lighthouses on Bodie Island and Hatteras Island. There's also a visitor center near the docks and boat ramp in Ocracoke Village. Water, rest rooms, and pay phones are available at each, as well as at campgrounds and in the small towns on the islands.

MAPS: See below under each of the 3 headings.

HAZARDS: The number one hazard at the national seashore is probably other boats. These tend to be concentrated around the 3 inlets—Oregon, Hatteras, and Ocracoke. Oregon Inlet in particular gets very crowded with fishing boats. Currents in these channels can be very unstable and difficult to negotiate. The currents off Cape Hatteras above Diamond Shoals deserve their reputation among mariners as some of the most treacherous on the East Coast.

PUT-INS/TAKE-OUTS: See below under each of the 3 separate headings.

Bodie Island

When discussing Bodie Island, a clarification is necessary: it isn't really an island at all. The inlet that once separated it from the rest of the barrier spit that runs north all the way into Virginia has

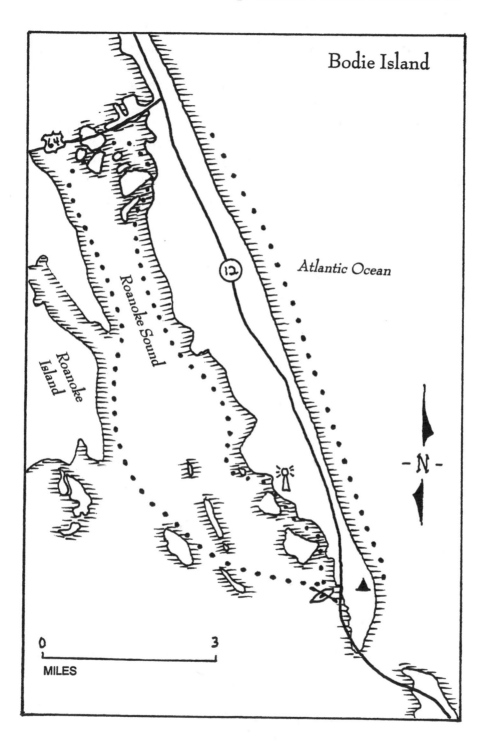

Bodie Island

Atlantic Ocean

Roanoke Sound

Roanoke Island

- N -

0   3

MILES

long since vanished. But the name remains. The "island" now refers to the land north of Oregon Inlet that's part of Cape Hatteras NS. Here is one of the few places in the seashore where the Outer Banks bulge to more than a mile across. Since the only highway access to the other islands begins here, most visitors start their trips by at least passing through. If you don't drive in on NC-12, the only other way to reach the national seashore is to take a ferry from the mainland to Ocracoke. Either because it's the entryway or because of its proximity to heavily developed Nags Head and Kill Devil Hills, Bodie Island always seems to be the busiest part of Cape Hatteras.

Like the other islands of the Cape Hatteras NS, Bodie has its landmark lighthouse. It was constructed in 1872 and is recognized by wide horizontal bands of black and white. Bodie's natural habitats are characteristic of the barrier islands that line the coast: a sand beach slopes upward to a buffer of sand dunes; behind the dunes are extensive sand flats that support thickets of various shrubs, with pockets of maritime forest; and on the sound side are marsh areas and tidal flats.

The shallow waters of Roanoke Sound—average depth is just 3 to 4 feet—are ideal for navigation in a sea kayak. Not only will you have the chance to explore the sound's marshes, islands, and coast up close, but boat traffic is relatively light, due to the location of the Intracoastal Waterway on the Alligator River to the west. And Roanoke Island has an important historical dimension worth exploring as well. It was here that the first permanent British settlement in North America was established. It didn't last of course, and what became of the inhabitants of the "Lost Colony" remains a mystery. The colony's 400th anniversary was recently celebrated; to commemorate it the *Elizabeth II*, a reproduction of the type of 16th-century sailing vessel used by Sir Walter Raleigh, was installed in the harbor at Manteo.

MAPS: NOAA chart 12205; USGS Oregon Inlet, Roanoke Island Northeast.

HAZARDS: Oregon Inlet poses the main hazard for kayakers. Hundreds of fishing vessels pass through each day during peak season on their way to offshore fishing grounds. And since it's the only inlet between Virginia and Cape Hatteras, an awful lot of water has to squeeze through during each change in tide, creating strong, dangerous currents.

BASE CAMP: Oregon Inlet campground is located near the S end of Bodie Island on the ocean side. It's run by the NPS and is open from mid-April to Labor Day. Sites cost $12/night. If you'd rather sleep in a bed, you'll find hotels, motels, B&Bs, and condos on Roanoke Island or just up the road in Nags Head.

PUT-IN: Boat ramps are at the Oregon Inlet Marina, located at the N end of the Herbert C. Bonner bridge. From the junction of US-64 and NC-12, drive S on NC-12 8 miles to the marina, R.

TAKE-OUT: Same as the put-in.

DAYTRIP: *Roanoke Sound Circuit. A 17-mile loop trip featuring the ecology of Roanoke Sound, the western shore of Bodie Island, and the eastern side of Roanoke Island. Difficulty rating: 3.*

From the put-in beside the Ocracoke Inlet marina, paddle up the sound side of Bodie Island, following the coastline. As you proceed, you'll have to navigate in and out of the numerous small islands that hug the shore. As you pass the Bodie Island lighthouse at 2 miles, the S tip of Roanoke Island will be due W. Keep to the shore of Bodie Island and paddle 6 miles up to the US-64 bridge that crosses the sound. Turn L and paddle to the E shore of Roanoke Island. (If you want to have a look at the Elizabeth II and Manteo Harbor from the water, paddle another mile N to Shallowbag Bay.) As you near the island, turn S and run parallel to the shore. When you reach the island's S end, veer SE and return to the put-in.

DAYTRIP 2: *Ocean Strand. An unstructured paddle of up to 16 miles on the ocean side of Bodie Island. Highlights include the wreck of the Laura*

Barnes and Coquina Beach. Difficulty rating: 4.

Put in from the beach at the Oregon Inlet campground or Coquina Beach. Paddle out past the breakers and turn NNW. Follow the coast in this direction as far as you want. It's a long uninterrupted stretch of sandy beach—perfect for practicing surfing or for taking a break for swimming or sunbathing. Just a short distance past the put-in, you'll pass the wreck of the Laura Barnes, visible on the beach. At 6.5 miles is the Outer Banks fishing pier. At 8 miles you'll reach the end of the NS. Turn around and retrace your route back to the campground.

Hatteras Island

The long, bent middle island of the national seashore is the one most people think of when they hear the words Cape Hatteras. It could be that the cape is actually on the island, right at the outer edge of the bend where the Outer Banks rotate from a north–south orientation to one that's more northeast–southwest. It could also be that the famed Cape Hatteras Lighthouse, constructed in 1870 to mark the treacherous waters above diamond shoals and the tallest lighthouse in the United States, is one of the most distinctive landmarks on the East Coast. Or it could just be that with 80 miles each of ocean beach and sound frontage offering some of the best fishing, swimming, and at-the-beach outdoor recreation in the nation, this is simply where most people visiting the national seashore end up.

The lay of the land is familiar to anyone who has spent time on a barrier island. Beach, dunes, shrub thickets, marsh, and tidal flats are the predominant habitats, laid end to end from sea to sound. Added to these is an extensive parcel of maritime forest, sheltered from harsh winds and sea spray on the backside of the island near Buxton and Cape Hatteras. A few small villages dot the island, sitting on the perimeter of federal land and providing easy access to facilities. At the northern end of the island is the Pea Island National Wildlife Refuge, a separate entity whose main

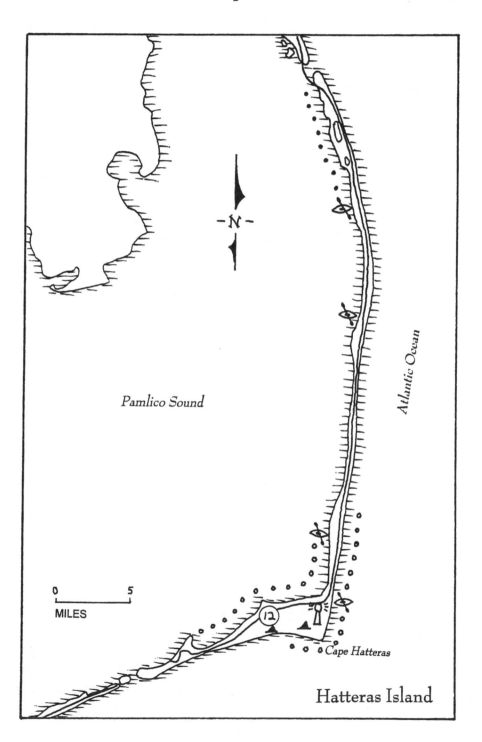

Atlantic Ocean

-N-

Pamlico Sound

0   5
MILES

12

Cape Hatteras

Hatteras Island

mission is to provide unspoiled habitat for migrating waterfowl and shore birds. This is one of the island's hot spots for dedicated bird watchers.

Although you certainly won't be alone no matter what time of year you visit Hatteras Island (except perhaps during a hurricane), with only minimal development on the island, you'll never really feel crowded, either. Surfers, swimmers, beachcombers, and sunbathers are drawn by the miles of sandy beach. Anglers come from all over the eastern seaboard and beyond to try their luck in the surf, sound, or on deep-sea expeditions offshore. Dozens of sport fish roam these waters at various times of year, including blues, Spanish and king mackerel, black and red drum, flounder, mullet, and trout, to name just a few.

Sea kayaking is relatively new to the mix of popular outdoor recreational activities on Hatteras Island, but it's quickly gaining a foothold. And with so many intriguing marine environments to explore and so many miles of unspoiled coast, it isn't surprising. The island is now dotted with outfitters renting kayaks and offering guided tours. The trips below are only two possibilities out of dozens. In truth, you could spend a week paddling the ocean and sound around Hatteras Island and not run out of new places to discover.

MAPS: NOAA charts 12204, 11555; USGS Pea Island, Rodanthe, Little Kinnakeet, Buxton, Cape Hatteras, Hatteras, Oregon Inlet.

HAZARDS: Hatteras Island has the most dangerous ocean currents on the national seashore. Diamond Shoals, just off the cape, has particularly treacherous conditions. And rip currents plague the island's entire length. Boat traffic and tricky currents are a problem in the inlets at either end of the island. Oregon Inlet in particular should be avoided. Hunting takes place on Pea Island NWR during fall and winter.

BASE CAMP: Campers can overnight at either of 2 ocean-side NPS campgrounds, Cape Point and Frisco. Both are located a short drive from the lighthouse and are open from Memorial Day to

Labor Day. Sites cost $12/night. There are also several private campgrounds on the islands. Hotels, motels, lodges, and B&Bs can be found in the handful of small towns that line Hatteras Island.

PUT-INS: Daytrip: A boat ramp is located in the Pea Island NWR at New Inlet. To get there, take NC-12 S 2.8 miles from the NWR visitor center. Access on the ocean side is just 0.2 miles N of the visitor center.

Weekender: A long strip of sand on the sound side at an area known as Canadian Hole is a popular spot for launching windsurfing boards and kayaks. To get there, drive N on NC-12 2.5 miles from the lighthouse access road. The parking lot is on the L.

Another sound-side put-in is located in the Salvo Day-Use area.

Beach access is located at numerous locations up and down the island. The put-in for day 2 of the weekender is near the lighthouse. From the beach access parking lot across from the lighthouse and visitor center, you have to portage about 200 yds across a boardwalk and the beach.

TAKE-OUT: Same as the put-ins.

DAYTRIP: *Refuge and Sound Exploration. This 14-mile round-trip begins and ends in the Pea Island NWR. It follows the back side of Hatteras Island and offers an excellent chance to observe the flora and fauna—particularly avian species—typical of a barrier island. Difficulty rating: 3.*

Put-in at New Inlet just off NC-12. Paddle N, following the coastline, but taking time to weave in and out of the islands and marshes that line Pamlico Sound's shoreline. Birds are abundant in the area, so you'll want to bring a pair of binoculars for observation. And if you bring rod and reel, you can cast for fish in the fertile waters of the sound. When you near Oregon Inlet, a distance of some 7 miles, turn around and paddle back down the coast. Return to the put-in at New Inlet.

WEEKENDER: *Sheltered Sound/Lighthouse Strand Combo. 2 separate day trips explore Pamlico Sound behind Buxton Woods and then the long stretch of Ocean in front of the Cape Hatteras Lighthouse. Overnight at one of the 2 NPS campgrounds in the area. Difficulty rating: 3, 5.*

The first half of the weekender charts a 20-mile course behind Buxton Woods and the lighthouse. Put in at Canadian Hole and follow the shoreline S about a mile to where the island bends sharply to the left at Buxton. As you turn W, you can observe Buxton Woods, the largest tract of maritime forest on the national seashore. Paddle 4 miles out along the shoreline past Kings Point and then veer slightly to the L and enter the semi-sheltered cove of Sandy Bay, which ends at Durant Point. Kings Point to Durant Point is a distance of 5 miles. When you reach the point, turn around and retrace your route back to the put-in at Canadian Hole.

Day 2 is a trip up and down the Atlantic Ocean coast N of the cape and the treacherous currents around Diamond Shoals. Highlights are the long sandy stretch of beach and dunes, the chance to observe dozens of species of shore birds, a possible swimming break, and of course, the landmark lighthouse. Put in just S of the lighthouse. Keep in mind that the surf here can get pretty rough and that this is a popular surfing and swimming area. If it's too crowded, put in at another beach access to the N. From the put-in, you can paddle as far as you want N, or head S and curve around the cape. Avoid the latter unless you're comfortable managing strong, unpredictable currents. On the other side of Cape Hatteras is Hatteras Cove, where the surf is considerably lighter. The take-out for this trip is the same as the put-in.

Ocracoke Island

Ocracoke, as they say, has a charm all its own. The 18-mile-long island has changed little over the centuries, with a pace and

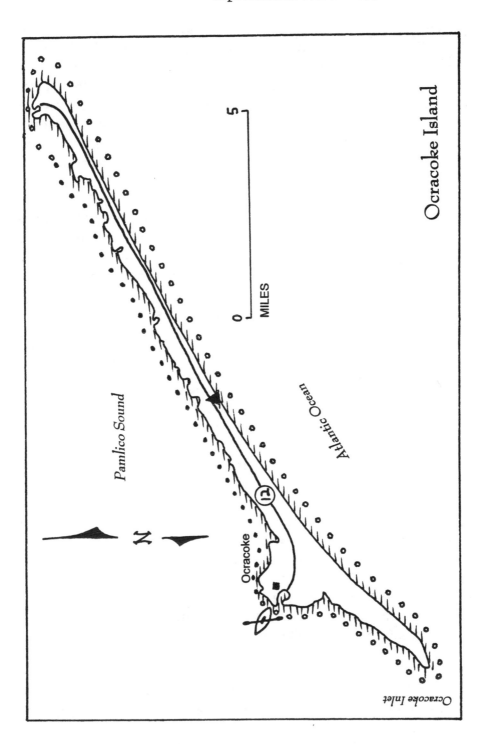

setting that don't seem to owe much to modern-day notions of progress. Much of the lazy, laid-back appeal of the small island is due to its out-of-the-way location. No matter how you get there, it's going to take a while. And the only way you can get there is by boat or ferry. From the mainland, its at least a 2-hour crossing from either Cedar Island or Swan Quarter. Another, 40-minute ferry, connects the island to Hatteras Island and the rest of the national seashore, but from there you have to drive 60 miles north to Roanoke Island and the interstate.

Ocracoke Island is rich in both history and ecology. By the time the English washed up on its sandy shores in 1585, Native Americans had been roving the waters that surround it in dugout canoes for centuries. Although the fate of the first English settlers to visit the island is not known, Queen Elizabeth liked the promise of the new land and soon sent additional parties to settle the island and surrounding coast. Ocracoke's isolation from the mainland and even from the rest of the Outer Banks resulted in patterns of livelihood and custom that changed little over the centuries. An oft-quoted fact is that TV didn't arrive until well into the 1980s. Even today traces of the cadences and inflections of Elizabethan English can be heard in the speech of native Ocracokers. One of the island's most infamous residents was the storied pirate Blackbeard, who attacked passing ships from Ocracoke's sheltered coves. He met his end here too, when he was captured and beheaded in a place know as Teach's Hole.

Some of the remnants of the island's earliest European residents can still be seen on the island—a small herd of wild ponies that's believed to be descended from Spanish stock. You'll see plenty of fauna that's truly native to the island as well. Just look along the beach, or on the waters of the sound, or overhead, and see how many of the 400 species of birds that have been observed on the Outer Banks you can count.

Although the island's wonderful natural habitats and the relaxed charm of Ocracoke Village are reasons enough for a visit, sea kayakers have added incentives. The same coves that provided cover for pirates are ideally explored from a kayak. And even with 3 ferry lines and sometimes scores of fishing vessels coming and going from the island, you'll rarely have any sense of being crowded. And Ocracoke's natural harbor, Silver Lake, is one of the most delightful places on the entire Outer Banks to spend a lazy morning or afternoon paddling. You can even pull up at the docks and stop in at one of the waterfront eateries for a quick snack.

Before heading out onto the water, you can stop by the NPS headquarters building (open seasonally) next to the ferry terminal. Current weather forecasts are available inside, and restrooms, water, and a pay phone are also there.

MAPS: NOAA charts 11550, 11555; USGS Green Island, Howard Reef, Ocracoke.

HAZARDS: Silver Lake Harbor is the busiest spot on the island, with fishing and pleasure boats coming and going throughout the day. The narrow inlet into the harbor is a particularly tight squeeze, especially if a ferry is making its way through too. Currents at the inlets on either end of Ocracoke Island are strong and unpredictable.

BASE CAMP: An NPS-run campground is located on the ocean side of Ocracoke Island. It's open from the middle of April to Labor Day. Sites cost $13/night. You can reserve a site (not a bad idea if you're coming during peak season) by calling 800/365-2267. If you want to spend more than a day on the island but would rather not camp, you'll find plenty of accommodations of various sorts in Ocracoke Village. Contact the Ocracoke Civic & Business Association (919/928-6711) for listings or other info.

PUT-IN: A boat ramp is located across the parking lot from the NPS visitor center at the S end of NC-12 (near the ferry terminal) in Ocracoke Village. Access to the beach is possible from numerous locations, including the campground.

TAKE-OUT: If you're traveling in one car, take out from the put-in, whether it's the boat ramp or beach. With 2 cars, one-way trips are possible, with one easy take-out on the beach next to the campground.

DAYTRIP: *The Coves of Ocracoke. A 20-mile, round-trip loop that explores the numerous coves that line Ocracoke Island's back coast. The trip begins and ends at the boat ramp in Ocracoke Village. Difficulty rating: 3.*

From the put-in next to the village ferry terminal, paddle E along the island's shoreline. From the water here you can look back over your shoulder and see the village and Ocracoke Lighthouse, the oldest operational lighthouse in the United States. The shore is sandy until you approach Quokes Point at 4 miles, where marsh begins to predominate. The tidal flats are quite broad along much of this side of the island; at low tide you'll have to paddle at a distance from the shoreline. Along the 7-mile stretch of island from the point to Green Island, the geography of the shoreline is broken up by numerous coves and several creeks. Set a leisurely pace and explore as many of these fascinating areas as you have time to. When you reach Green Island, turn N and paddle the short distance to Outer Green Island. Circle the island and retrace your route back to the boat ramp.

WEEKENDER: *Ocracoke Island Circumnavigation. A 37-mile trip that begins and ends in Ocracoke Village, with an overnight at the oceanside campground. Difficulty rating: 4.*

On day 1, put in at the boat ramp next to the ferry slips. Paddle SW away from Gap Point to Silver Lake Harbor. Duck into the harbor for a quick circuit to check out the fishing boats and the buildings of Ocracoke Village. Included among these is the Ocracoke Lighthouse, operational since 1823. When you leave the harbor, turn S and stick close to shore as you paddle toward Ocracoke Inlet. Watch out for ferry and fishing boat traffic in the area. Most of this part of the island has a sandy shoreline backed up by shrub thicket and pockets of live oaks. After 4 miles come to Ocracoke Inlet. If the current is more than you want to handle, land on the back side of the beach and portage around to the front side. When you reach the ocean, paddle ENE along one of the most delightful stretches of sandy beach in the state. After 8 miles come to the campground.

Day 2 covers 24 miles, so plan on a full day of paddling. Put in on the beach and paddle out beyond the surf. Turn ENE and follow the sandy coastline to Hatteras Inlet, 8.5 miles away. The conflicting currents of the inlet are not for the faint of heart. You can portage around it, but it's a hike to do so. Also keep an eye out for the Hatteras–Ocracoke Ferry. Since one leaves every half-hour in summer, they always seem to be passing by. When you reach Pamlico Sound, follow the line of the island WSW. If you're in the mood for exploring, this is the place to do it. Coves, creeks, and small islands line this part of the sound's shoreline, inviting curious paddlers. Keep in mind that it's a 14-mile paddle from the inlet to the take-out just past Gap Point.

Mattamuskeet National Wildlife Refuge

Lake Mattamuskeet

North Carolina's largest natural lake offers paddlers one of the most unusual and exhilarating natural environments in the state to explore. The lake, marshes, and forests that comprise the refuge are nationally famous for the vast numbers of geese, swans, and ducks they attract every fall and winter.

The origins of the lake are uncertain, but one thing that is known is that it is a relatively recent addition to the area's topography. Mattamuskeet is an Algonquin word that means "dry dust," a designation that hardly fits a body of water that measures 18 miles long and 6 miles wide. Whether the lake was formed by a vast fire or by some other means, it probably wasn't here when the Indians' earliest ancestors hunted the fields and forests that stood in its place.

The lake almost didn't survive into the present. Beginning in 1914, plans on a massive scale were put in place to drain the 40,000-acre lake and convert it into productive farmland. A few obstacles to these plans were considerable, including the fact that the lake is several feet *below* sea level. Nevertheless, a thousand miles of canals were built—the company responsible took the apt name New Holland Farms—and the world's largest pumps were prepared to divert the water. Despite the bankruptcies of several companies involved in the project, in 1928 the lake was drained and for 5 years it was the site of one of the most productive farms in the nation. A town—dubbed New Holland—was built, and a railroad line laid down. Then the rains came. Despite their vast capacity, the pumps could not handle the excess load and failed. The following year a 50,000-acre tract that included the lake and surrounding land was sold to the federal government, which in turn used the acreage for a wildlife refuge.

Although the remains of the derelict pumps and pump house can still be seen and are on the National Register of Historic

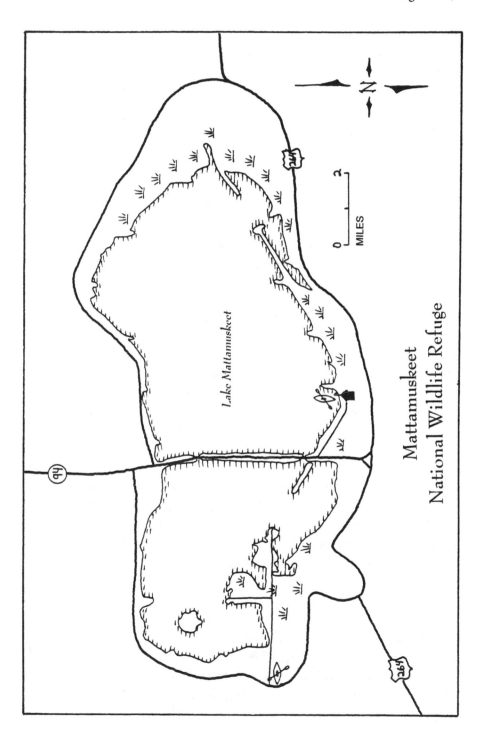

Mattamuskeet
National Wildlife Refuge

Places, most visitors to the refuge come to observe the thousands upon thousands of waterfowl that use the lake. The numbers defy exaggeration. On an average winter day, 110,000 ducks, 35,000 tundra swans, 12,000 Canada geese, and 5,000 snow geese can be seen on the lake. Although the fall and winter months are the best times of year to observe the lake's wildlife, the lake is open to boaters only between March 1 and November 1. Despite the limitation, which is for the protection of the migrating waterfowl, plenty of the more than 200 avian species that have been observed at Mattamuskeet are common throughout the year. Ospreys, kestrels, great blue herons, egrets, and cormorants (to name just a few) are all regularly seen. Bald eagles are sometimes spotted in winter and early spring. Mammals that inhabit the refuge include white-tailed deer, river otter, and bobcat. You may catch a glimpse of them in the marshes or forest that line Mattamuskeet's perimeter. If you have any interest in wildlife photography, be sure to bring a camera with a zoom lens.

Mattamuskeet presents sea kayakers with a few conditions that are rather unusual for a coastal environment. First, despite the lake's immense proportions, it is the shallowest in North Carolina, with an average depth of just over 2 feet. This keeps all boats but those with the shallowest drafts off the lake. You'll never have to contend with sailboats or pleasure cruisers. On many days, it's possible to paddle in virtual isolation—except for the wildlife, of course. Second, although storms and stiff winds are not unheard of, the lake generally offers paddlers one of the most serene bodies of water on the coast. The constant driving wind and choppy waters often encountered on the sounds are relatively rare here. Since camping isn't permitted on the refuge, daytrips only are possible.

INFORMATION: Mattamuskeet National Wildlife Refuge, Route 1, Box N-2, Swanquarter, NC 27885; 919/926-4021. A refuge map and brochure and wildlife checklists are available at the refuge HQ. Water and rest rooms are also there. During the warm months you can rent a kayak out back too.

MAPS: USGS New Holland, Fairfield, Engelhard West, Middletown, Swanquarter, New Lake Southeast.

BASE CAMP: Camping is not allowed on the refuge, and the hunting lodge that once operated in the main pump house has been out of use since 1974. Although this limits overnight options, you can camp at the Riverside Campground (919/943-2849), a private campground located between the lake and Belhaven. A state campground is located in Pettigrew State Park on Lake Phelps (see separate entry above). A couple of lodges and inns are located in Belhaven.

PUT-IN/TAKE-OUT: There are 3 boat ramps on the lake. To reach the put-in for daytrip 1: from the junction of US-264 and NC-94, drive N on NC-94 1.5 miles to the refuge entrance. Turn R and go 2 miles on the gravel road to the refuge HQ. The boat ramp is behind the building.

To reach the put-in for daytrip 2: From the main refuge access road, turn S onto NC-94 and go 1.5 miles to US-264. Turn R and go 5.6 miles to SR-1304. Turn R and go 4.7 miles to the boat ramp access road, R. Turn R and go 0.2 miles to the boat ramp.

The 3rd boat ramp is located on NC-94 just N of the refuge access road.

DAYTRIP 1: *East End Exploration. An unstructured paddle that begins in the canals on the lake's S shore and covers as much of the eastern half of the lake as you feel like paddling. Difficulty rating: 1.*

One of the unusual features of Lake Mattamuskeet is that you can only paddle half of it at a time. The embankment that NC-94 runs on effectively cuts the lake in half, although water can pass through in tunnels too small for kayaks.

Put in behind the visitor center. Paddle E along the canal a short distance (less than 50 yds) to an intersecting canal. Turn L and paddle under the bridge and up the canal to the lake. Once you reach the lake, you can chart whatever course you like. All areas of the lake are accessible to kayaks. The main attractions are the marshes and pockets of forest along the shore (and in some places mid-lake), and of course the diversity and vast numbers of birds.

DAYTRIP 2: *West End Exploration. A paddle around the marsh islands and wooded shoreline of the lake's smaller half. Highlights include extensive marsh areas. Difficulty rating: 1.*

The lack of camping facilities on the refuge and its daylight-only hours mean that multi-day trips must be pieced together with a series of daytrips. This may require a little extra effort on your part, but you'll be amply rewarded by the extra time you spend in the vast, magical environment of Mattamuskeet. Really, the lake's size makes it impossible to fully explore or appreciate in a single day.

Since NC-94 divides the lake almost in half, paddling half of the lake one day and the other half the next day is a natural way to break up a weekend trip. This daytrip explores the lake's smaller, western section. From the put-in described above, Paddle E through the long canal 2.5 miles to an intersecting canal on the L. Turn into the other canal and paddle 1 mile to where it empties into the lake. From there, choose your own route. You'll probably want to explore the regions around Great Island and Head Lake Island. When you're ready to return, retrace your route through the canals to the put-in.

Goose Creek State Park

Goose Creek ◊ Pamlico River ◊ Bath Creek

Goose Creek State Park is located in a region of the North Carolina coastal plain as appealing for its easygoing charm and historical significance as for the beauty of its natural environments. The 1,600-acre park sits at the confluence of the eponymous creek and the Pamlico River in Beaufort County. Although much of the surrounding countryside has been altered by agriculture—tobacco is the main crop—the park preserves some of the natural habitats that are native to the area.

Since early colonial times, the region's fertile soil has attracted planters. But it was the waterways and natural harbors that made the north shore of the Pamlico River such an important commercial center during the 18th and into the 19th centuries. The Pamlico River provided easy access to Pamlico Sound, Ocracoke Inlet, and the Atlantic Ocean. A natural harbor on Bath Creek became the site of the state's first official port and its first incorporated town. Bath came into existence on March 8, 1705, and although it had only a handful of dwellings, its port soon became a busy commercial and government center. Although the population of Bath has never exceeded more than a few hundred people, among those who lived there in its earliest days were royal governors, traders, and the infamous pirate Blackbeard.

The town's fortunes waned as other, larger ports opened on the coastal plain, and today its main significance is historical. You can see some of the six-block historical district from the water, or land at the waterfront park and stroll among the preserved buildings that recall North Carolina's earliest days. Located here are St. Paul's Church (1734) and the Palmer-Marsh house, the state's oldest church and one of its oldest residences, a building once used as a meeting place for the General Assembly.

Fifteen miles upriver from Bath is another old town with historical importance and a unique claim to fame: it was the first

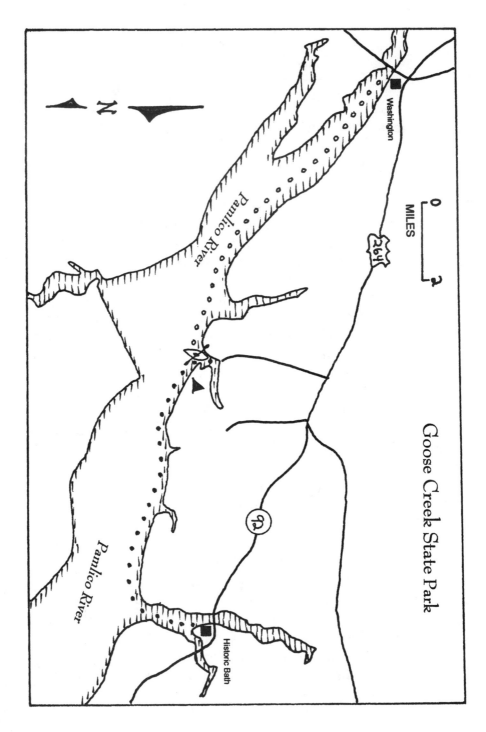

town in the United States named after George Washington. Like Bath, but somewhat larger, Washington has a historic district that can be viewed from the water or wandered on foot. The waterfront has undergone extensive renovation in the past few decades, and now a pleasant park area lies between the river and buildings that date from the early 19th century. Although Washington wasn't established until almost 70 years after Bath, it quickly eclipsed it in importance and became a leading port in its own right.

Before English settlers lived in the area, the region around the Pamlico and Tar Rivers was home to two Tuscarora Indian tribes, the Secotan and Pamlico. At that time most of the surrounding area was a dense, nearly impenetrable wilderness of swamp forest and shrub thickets known as pocosins. Remnants of these habitats can still be observed as you paddle the waters of Goose Creek and the Pamlico River past the state park. Other habitats include brackish marshes and upland forest. At the water's edge live oaks and pines draped with Spanish moss provide a picturesque paddling environment. Birds—both migratory and year-round residents—take advantage of the park's natural habitats. Herons, egrets, swans, geese, ducks, and hawks are just some of the species you might encounter as you paddle the river and creeks.

For a region that grew to prominence because of its waterways, a kayak is the perfect means of exploration. After all, the towns and settlements in the area grew up around the Pamlico River and the smaller creeks that feed it, so arriving at them from the water is only natural. If you want to change pace, however, and try some other outdoor recreation, you'll find opportunities for hiking, birding, and nature study in the state park, as well as a small campground. And of course fishing has been a popular and commercially important activity here for at least a couple of centuries. Since the Pamlico is a tidal river, you can angle for both saltwater and freshwater fish.

INFORMATION: Superintendent, Goose Creek State Park, Route 2, Box 372, Washington, NC 27889; 919/923-2191. If you're interested in exploring more of the park than just its waterways, stop by the park office and pick up a trail map and brochure. They can also fill you in on current conditions. Water and restrooms are located at the office and near the swimming beach.

MAPS: NOAA chart 11554; USGS Blounts Bay, Bath, Washington.

HAZARDS: The Pamlico River is one of the major water routes on the coastal plain. Although boats of all sorts ply its waters, the routes described below follow the shoreline closely enough so that they're out of the main channels. Wakes and open water conditions should be anticipated on the river.

BASECAMP: If you want to spend more than a day exploring the area, the park campground makes the perfect base for an overnight trip. 12 large sites are situated in a sparsely wooded area near Goose Creek and the Pamlico River. The views are superb and there's a boat launch area right in the campground. If you'd prefer a room in a hotel or motel, you'll find a selection in nearby Washington. Contact the Washington Chamber of Commerce (919/946-9168) for listings or other info.

PUT-IN: From Washington, take US-264 E 9 miles to Camp Leach Rd (SR-1334). Turn R and go 2.1 miles to the park entrance. The weekender put-in is at the campground. There's a small parking area at sites #11 & 12, from which a short portage is necessary to put in on Goose Creek.

For the daytrip, leave the park and drive back out Camp Leach Rd 2.1 miles to US-264. Turn L and go 1.1 miles to Goose Creek Rd. Turn L and go 2.7 miles (at 0.6 miles the pavement ends) to the end of the road and boat launch.

TAKE-OUT: Same as the put-ins above.

DAYTRIP: *A Paddle Back in Time. A 16-mile round-trip paddle that follows the Pamlico River downstream to Bath Creek and Historic Bath. Highlights include the colonial architecture of the state's oldest town and the natural habitats along the shoreline. Difficulty rating: 2.*

From the boat ramp, paddle out Goose Creek the short distance to the Pamlico River. Turn L and follow the river's north shore. This is a good place to observe the park's natural habitats and do some bird-watching. After a mile or 2 there's a sandy beach and a picnic area that makes a nice place for a break or a snack. Pass a couple of small creeks and at 6 miles come to Bath Creek on the L. Turn into the creek and paddle 2 miles N to where the small town appears on the R. At this point you may wish to get out and have lunch or just look around the historic downtown area (taking out on the waterfront is no problem, just paddle around to the back side of Bonnet Point Park), or continue paddling up the scenic creek. When you're ready to return, retrace your route back to the SP.

WEEKENDER: *Up & Down the Pamlico into History. 2 daytrips with an overnight at the Goose Creek SP campground. The first day's route follows the river upstream to where it narrows at Washington. And on the second day the route changes directions and heads downriver to Historic Bath. Difficulty rating: 2.*

From the campground put-in, paddle to the mouth of Goose Creek and the wide, tidal Pamlico River. Turn R and follow the river upstream. At 1 mile pass the mouth of Broad Creek. If you have rod and reel, you may want to spend some time casting into the mouths of either of these creeks. Continue paddling along the river's N shoreline for 7 miles until you reach the Washington waterfront. Although there's a narrow waterfront park, it really isn't designed for easy access from the water. Circle the island known as The Castle in the middle of the river. When you're finished exploring the waterfront area, retrace your route back to the put-in.

On the second day, follow the daytrip route described above downriver to Historic Bath.

Cedar Island National Wildlife Refuge

Pamlico Sound ◊ Core Sound

To the observer passing through on NC-12, Cedar Island seems like a coastal version of Kansas. Table-top flat, with acre upon acre of narrow golden reeds that stretch to the horizon and glisten in the sun. Not wheat of course, but black needlerush salt marsh. And passing through is just how most visitors see the Cedar Island National Wildlife Refuge: driving to the ferry terminal to get to Ocracoke. Which makes sense, since the refuge is at the end of the road—NC-12 to be exact. Unless you're actually coming to visit the refuge, or passing through on the way to the Outer Banks, or just plain lost, odds are very good that you won't end up in this out-of-the-way natural preserve.

If you do come to visit this magnificent, 13,000-acre expanse of saltwater marsh (the largest in the state) and pine forest, you won't find much in the way of improvements except that narrow ribbon of asphalt. The refuge is managed primarily to provide habitat for waterfowl migrating along the Atlantic Flyway. Cedar Island sits at the end of a large peninsula that juts out into Pamlico Sound. It's separated from the mainland by a narrow cut that connects the waters of Pamlico Sound and Core Sound, waters that are responsible for more than 80% of the refuge being marsh.

A kayak is a perfect vessel to get around Cedar Island in, since the lack of firm uplands means that most of the refuge is inaccessible from a car or on foot. And the stealth of a kayak will allow you to observe up-close some of the nearly 300 species of birds that have been observed on Cedar Island. The winter months are best for viewing migratory species, but avid bird watchers won't leave disappointed at any time of year. Some of the more abundant or commonly seen species are the common loon, green heron, cattle egret, black duck, wood duck, harrier, clapper rail, black rail, black skimmer, and the belted kingfisher. A complete

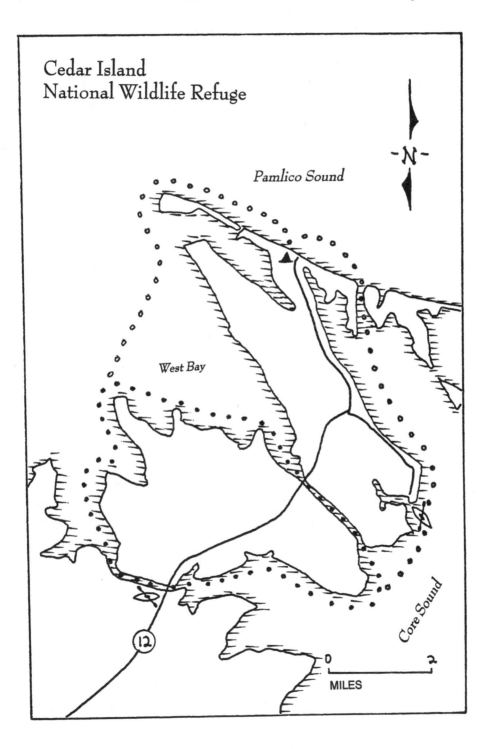

Cedar Island
National Wildlife Refuge

-N-

Pamlico Sound

West Bay

Core Sound

12

0   2
MILES

bird list is available from the refuge headquarters listed below. In addition to the birds, you might spot some porpoises; they're known to frequent these waters.

One of the main advantages of Cedar Island's out-of-the-way location is the opportunity for solitude it affords. Except for the occasional ferries leaving from the end of the island for Ocracoke, and the odd angler or two, chances are good that you won't have much company as you paddle around the refuge's edges. Most of what you'll see is marsh and water. The sameness of the vista may take some getting used to, but after awhile the marsh's austere environment takes on an appeal all its own. There is an abundance to it's seeming emptiness that's not unlike that of a desert.

Since camping isn't permitted on the refuge and it's open during daylight hours only, you'll have to experience it in daytrip-sized pieces, or combine a visit with a backcountry camping expedition to Core Banks on the Cape Lookout National Seashore. Since it's only about a 3-mile paddle across Core Sound, that's an excellent option for a single overnight or an extended exploration that takes in both the refuge and national seashore.

INFORMATION: Cedar Island National Wildlife Refuge, Route 1, Box N-2, Swan Quarter, NC 27885; 919/926-4021. The refuge HQ that still shows up on some maps was closed several years ago, the victim of federal budget cuts. There's no source of information on the refuge, and no facilities of any kind. The nearest water and restrooms are at the ferry terminal or in the small town of Atlantic.

MAPS: NOAA chart 11550; USGS Atlantic, North Bay.

HAZARDS: If you're paddling at the N end of the refuge, keep an eye out for ferries. Commercial fishing boats are a presence in Core Sound, but traffic is not heavy.

BASE CAMP: Although camping isn't allowed on the NWR, you can paddle across Core Sound (3–4 miles) and camp anywhere on the

Cape Lookout National Seashore. If you'd rather stay on the mainland, you'll find car campgrounds in Sea Level and at the ferry terminal. There's also a hotel in each location.

PUT-IN: From Beaufort, take US-70 N 25 miles to the junction with NC-12. Turn onto NC-12 and drive 2.7 miles to an access road just before the Gaskill Memorial Bridge. The boat ramp is at the end of the short road.

TAKE-OUT: Same as the put-in.

DAYTRIP: *The Bays of Cedar Island. A 15-mile loop that explores both the east and west side of the refuge, which are connected by a pair of canals. Highlights are salt marsh habitats and wilderness isolation. Difficulty rating: 3.*

Put in just before the high-rise bridge across the canal known as the Thorofare. Paddle W out the Thorofare 1 mile into West Thorofare Bay. Although the waters of this and the other bays of the trip are relatively sheltered, conditions can still get quite rough when the wind is up. Follow the curve of the marshes around to the R, entering and exiting a series of bays: Merkle Bay, Deep Bend, Nameless Bay, and finally the head of the larger West Bay. If you paddle a straight line across the mouth of these bays, the distance is 8 miles. Following the shoreline closely adds 3 to 4 miles. Enter a narrow cut called John Day's Ditch. This 1.75-mile canal connects the waters of Pamlico Sound and Core Sound and cuts the refuge in half. If the water's up you'll have to portage across NC-12, which passes over the ditch on a low bridge. At the end of the ditch reach Rumley Bay. Paddle less than a mile SE to the wooded parcel called Rumley Hammock. There's a long sandy landing here that makes the scenic area a nice spot for lunch or a break. After lunch, paddle W into Thorofare Bay. Continue 4 miles to its head at the Thorofare and put-in.

WEEKENDER: *Cedar Island Circumnavigation. A 21-mile paddle around the perimeter of the refuge, with an overnight at the Driftwood Campground next to the ferry terminal. This trip affords the opportu-*

nity to paddle for a couple of days through remote natural habitats. Difficulty rating: 3.

On day 1, put in at the boat ramp on the Thorofare. Paddle W 1 mile to West Thorofare Bay. Turn NW and paddle 2 miles to the bay's mouth. Turn N and head for Tump Point, 1 mile away at the bottom of West Bay. From there, veer NNE and paddle 3 miles across open water to Western Point. Turn NW and paddle out around Point of Grass at the extreme edge of the refuge. Once you've rounded the point, it's a 3-mile paddle ESE along the shoreline to the ferry terminal and campground (open seasonally). If you'd rather sleep in a bed, you can get a room at the next-door Driftwood Motel. Keep an eye out for ferry traffic in the area.

On day 2 begin by continuing your route ESE along the northernmost edge of the refuge. After a mile come to Ship Point. Turn S and paddle through a channel to Cedar Island Bay. Paddle 3 miles SE to the mouth of the bay. Turn SSW and follow the refuge's shoreline on Core Sound. After 2.5 miles reach Rumley Hammock. Turn W into Thorofare Bay and paddle 4 miles to the take-out on the Thorofare.

Cape Lookout National Seashore
Core Sound ◊ Back Sound ◊ Atlantic Ocean

For coastal kayakers, Cape Lookout National Seashore is North Carolina's version of Mecca. Nowhere else on the southeast coast will you encounter such a long, uninterrupted string of pristine barrier islands. And nowhere else will you be able to paddle for so many miles and not encounter any of the trappings of civilization.

The three main islands—North Core Banks, South Core Banks, and Shackleford Banks—line up along the mainland coast in a shape that resembles a check mark. Together they stretch for 55 miles from the eastern end of Bogue Banks all the way to the southern tip of Ocracoke Island. And not a single road, hotel, fast-food joint, or strip mall mars their natural beauty. In fact, the only way to reach the islands is by boat. And once you're there, about the only structures you'll find are a famous lighthouse, a small visitor center/museum, some fishermen's shacks, and the abandoned village of Portsmouth at the northern tip of North Core Banks. With distances from the mainland that range from one to three miles, the islands are ideally situated for being reached by short paddles across the sounds. And with so many miles of Atlantic coast and sound, they're the perfect destination for more ambitious paddlers looking to undertake multi-day expeditions.

The lighthouse that sits near the promontory of Cape Lookout was erected in 1859. Its mission was grave: to warn ships of the treacherous shoals just off the coast. Over the years these perilous waters claimed dozens of ships and hundreds of lives, earning the spit of land the ominous moniker *Promontorium Tremendum*, horrible headland. Although the lighthouse is closed to the public, its light continues to burn and its pattern of black and white diamonds is a familiar landmark of the Carolina coast. Equally well-known is the herd of feral horses that inhabits Shackleford Banks. The horses were left behind by settlers who eventually abandoned the island's harsh conditions for greener pastures.

The islands themselves are classic examples of the long, narrow, ever-shifting barrier islands that act as a buffer between the Atlantic Ocean and the North Carolina mainland. The wind and weather that have shaped and reshaped the islands over the centuries continue to work their ineluctable effects: dunes rise and fall, inlets open and close, and the islands continue to slowly migrate south and west. Although these processes are usually almost imperceptible, occurring over decades and centuries, when a violent storm hits, the islands' geography can change overnight.

Most days, however, the islands that comprise Cape Lookout NS are delightfully stable. A seemingly endless sand beach fronts the Atlantic Ocean. Behind it is a large network of dunes, anchored in place by sea grasses and shrub thicket. In a few places with sufficient shelter from wind and sea spray, pockets of maritime forest have gained a foothold. On the sound side are wide tidal flats and salt-water marshes. These habitats are a paradise for bird-watchers. At times the sky seems filled with brown pelicans, or laughing gulls, or migrating ducks. And the shallow waters on the islands' sound side are an important incubator for all kinds of marine life. The nearly constant presence of fishing boats of all shapes and sizes attests to that.

For paddlers, however, other boats are of only minor concern. The sheer size of the area and the shallowness of much of the water in the sounds keeps the fishing and pleasure boats concentrated in relatively narrow channels. That leaves the kayaker plenty of room to explore the intriguing world of the islands and their marine environment. The surf and sounds offer some of the best fishing on the East Coast. In the ocean, you might catch bluefish, mullet, pompano, red drum, black drum, puppy drum, or sea trout. In the sounds, clamming and crabbing are popular activities, as is gigging for flounder.

When you travel to Cape Lookout, be prepared for primitive conditions. You won't find much in the way of amenities on the islands. Apart from rest rooms at the visitor center on S Core Banks, in fact, you won't find any facilities at all. There's a hand water pump nearby, but it isn't always reliable; bring whatever water you'll need during a visit. Insect repellent is a must from April to October. And with almost no shade anywhere on the islands, you'll want to bring a strong sunscreen too. If you're camping, be sure to bring a tent with extra long stakes for anchoring in shifting sands. Although campfires are permitted below the high-tide line, a small stove is more eco-friendly.

INFORMATION: Cape Lookout National Seashore, 131 Charles St, Harkers Island, NC 28531; 919/728-2250. The new HQ building on Harkers Island is a good place to start a visit to the NS. Not only can you check on current weather and tide conditions, but they can provide you with maps, suggest camping sites, and answer any questions you might have. It's also a good place to fill up with water. Rest rooms and a pay phone are at the site too.

MAPS: Maps are listed below under each of the 3 separate sections.

HAZARDS: Fishing boats and pleasure cruisers are a common presence around Cape Lookout and in Barden Inlet and Lighthouse Channel. You can avoid them by sticking to the shallower flats outside the main channels. Other hazards are listed below under each of the 3 sections.

BASE CAMP: Primitive backcountry camping is permitted anywhere on the islands except within 100 feet of any structure. This makes Cape Lookout one of the best destinations along the NC coast for a weekend trip or expedition. There are no developed camping facilities on the seashore, however, so be sure to bring whatever you need, including plenty of water. If you would rather stay on the mainland, the closest hotels, motels, B&Bs and rental cottages are in Beaufort and on Bogue Banks.

PUT-INS/TAKE-OUTS: See below under each of the 3 separate headings.

North Core Banks

In relation to the mainland and populated areas, North Core Banks is the most remote and isolated portion of the Cape Lookout National Seashore. That wasn't always the case, however. In fact, the northern tip of the island was the location of Portsmouth Village, established in 1753 as a way station for cargo ships and populated into the twentieth century. Today the village is a ghost town, but the attractive buildings and lanes still remain. A self-guided tour through the village makes this one of the most popular stopping-off places in the national seashore. The fact that it's located only a short boat ride away from the popular village of Ocracoke adds to its popularity.

South of Portsmouth Village, the long, narrow island stretches for almost 20 miles. Once you get away from the village, the island is much like any other uninhabited barrier island on the Outer Banks. Miles of sandy beach stretch along the Atlantic coast, an extensive dune system is held in place by sea grasses and shrub thickets, and tidal flats and salt-water marsh line the island on its sound side. Tidal flats comprise a much larger segment of the ecology here than elsewhere on the national seashore.

Despite its remote location, North Core Banks is easily accessible by kayak. The southern half of the island can be reached from put-ins on the mainland, and the northern end can be reached by paddling across Ocracoke Inlet from Ocracoke Village. This will give you the opportunity to explore both a small island community that still thrives, and one that succumbed to the harsh conditions that are a part of life on the Outer Banks.

MAPS: NOAA chart 11550; USGS Portsmouth, Wainwright Island, Styron Bay.

HAZARDS: Ocracoke Inlet is the most heavily trafficked area around N Core Banks, especially considering that 3 different ferry lines enter Ocracoke Village. The currents in the Ocracoke Inlet strong and unpredictable.

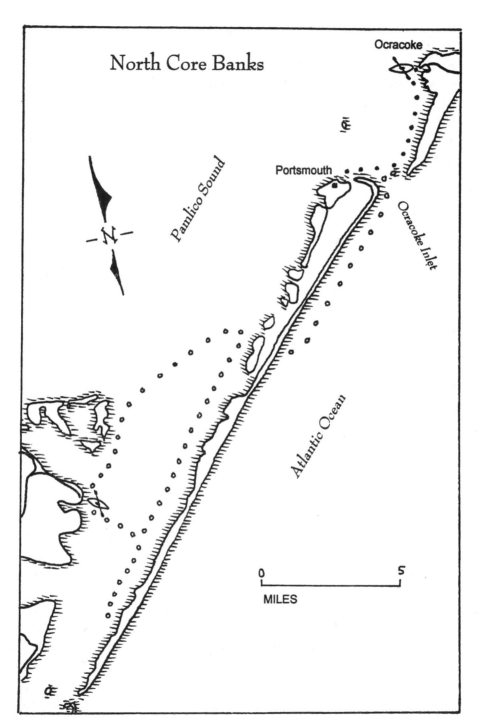

North Core Banks

Ocracoke

Pamlico Sound

Portsmouth

Ocracoke Inlet

Atlantic Ocean

0   5

MILES

BASE CAMP: Primitive backcountry camping is permitted anywhere on N Core Banks, except within 100 feet of any structure. A developed national park campground is on Ocracoke Island. It's open from mid-April to Labor Day. Ocracoke Village offers a good selection of overnight accommodations, including hotels, B&Bs, and cottages available for weekly rental. On the mainland, there's a campground and hotel at the Cedar Island ferry terminal, and one of each in Sealevel too.

PUT-INS: You can reach N Core Banks from Ocracoke Island or from the mainland. The daytrip and weekender 2 described below begin in Ocracoke. The weekender 1 trip begins on the mainland. The only way to get to Ocracoke is by ferry. There are 2 of them: A short (40 min), free ferry leaves from Hatteras Island, and ferries from the mainland leave from Swan Quarter and Cedar Island. Call 800/BY FERRY for schedules and rates. The kayak put-in is next to the Cape Hatteras NS info center at the end of NC-12 in Ocracoke.

On the mainland, you can put in at the Cedar Island NWR. From Beaufort, drive N on US-70 25 miles to NC-12. Turn L and go 8.2 miles to Lola Rd. Turn R and go 2.3 miles to the end of the road and the boat ramp.

TAKE-OUT: All 3 trips end where they begin.

DAYTRIP: *Village to Village. This 11-mi loop paddle takes in the sights of Silver Lake at Ocracoke Village and Portsmouth Village on Core Banks. The crossing of Ocracoke Inlet and open water conditions put it beyond the abilities of novice paddlers. Difficulty rating: 4*

From the put-in at the public boat ramp in Ocracoke, you can start your trip with a short detour to circle Silver Lake Harbor. Paddle E 400 yds to the harbor entrance. Turn L and enter through the ditch. The still waters of the harbor, lined with docks, shops, vacation homes, and restaurants, is the heart of Ocracoke Village. After you've circled the harbor, exit and paddle SW along the island's sound-side coast 4 miles to Ocracoke Inlet. Paddle 1 mile across the inlet and follow the arc of N Core Banks around to the sound side and Portsmouth Village. You can beach your kayak not far from the village. Spend some time exploring the relict church, school, and cemetery of the ghost town. If you want to spend time on the beach, you'll have to paddle to get there; tidal flats separate the village from the ocean and sand. To return to Ocracoke Island and the take-out, retrace your route.

WEEKENDER 1: *Core Sound Exploration. An unstructured 10–40 mile round trip paddle up and down the sound side of N Core Banks. Highlights are the remote locations and the pristine barrier island. Difficulty rating: 3.*

From the put-in at the end of Lola Rd in the Cedar Island NWR, paddle ESE across Core Sound. At 2.75 miles you'll reach the island. Turn SSW and follow its shoreline to a sandy landing 3 miles S. This is the best natural landing on the island, since most of the rest of the shoreline is salt marsh. Make camp somewhere in the vicinity. On the second day, follow the island NNE. Portsmouth Village is 18 miles N. Don't try to reach it, unless you're willing to paddle 30 miles in a single day or are going to camp a second night on the island. When you've explored as much of Core Sound and the island as you want, paddle back across the open water to the put-in.

WEEKENDER 2: *Portsmouth Village/Ocean Strand Combo. Beginning in Ocracoke, this 15–45-mile round-trip visits the abandoned town of Portsmouth before a long paddle along the Atlantic shore of N Core Banks. Difficulty rating: 5.*

Begin the trip by paddling S and SW along the Pamlico Sound coast of Ocracoke Island. After 4 miles reach Ocracoke Inlet. Cross the inlet behind the breakers and follow the curve of N Core Banks W to the village of Portsmouth, 3 miles away. After you've explored the village, paddle back around to the ocean side of the island and turn SW. The coast runs in a straight line for 16 miles to New Drum Inlet. You can tailor your trip by paddling as much of this distance as you like before making camp on the beach.

On the second day, simply retrace your path back to Ocracoke Village. Try to leave enough time for at least a short paddle around the serene waters of Silver Lake Harbor, the prettiest natural anchorage on the Outer Banks.

South Core Banks

South Core Banks is the site of the lighthouse and the infamous Cape Lookout. Both are located at the bottom of the 22-mile island. The latter curves around in a sandy hook at the back side of the island, where it turns north toward Shackleford Banks. Just offshore of the cape is the treacherous Frying Pan Shoals, which earned for the cape its designation on 16th century maps: *Promontorium Tremendum*, horrible headland.

Visitors to South Core Banks can usually be found bunched up around the lighthouse. The ferry landing is nearby, as is the museum/visitor center. Sun shelters with picnic tables clustered there provide respite from the sun. North of the cape and lighthouse, the only structures to be found on the long, narrow island are some fishermen's cabins.

With no inlets along the island's length, kayakers have to commit to paddling the shallow, relatively calm waters of the sound, or venturing through New Drum Inlet or around Cape Lookout to the open waters of the Atlantic. Currents around the cape are some of the most treacherous on the East Coast—novice paddlers should avoid this region entirely, and even experienced hands would be well advised to exercise extreme caution.

MAPS: NOAA charts 11545, 11544; USGS Horsepen Point, Davis, Styron bay, Harkers Island, Cape Lookout, Atlantic.

HAZARDS: Barden Inlet has the most boat traffic in this part of the NS. The currents around Cape Lookout are dangerous during even the best conditions. The remote, deserted location of most of S Core Banks demands that extra precautions be taken.

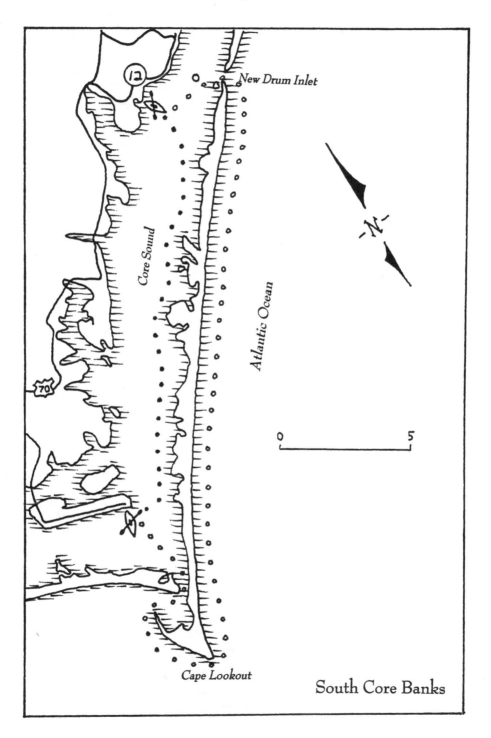

New Drum Inlet

Core Sound

Atlantic Ocean

N

0   5

Cape Lookout

South Core Banks

BASE CAMP: Primitive backcountry camping is permitted anywhere on the island, except within 100 feet of a structure. A private campground is located next to the boat ramp in Sealevel. If you'd rather not camp, you can overnight in the one hotel in Sealevel. A larger variety of accommodations is available in Beaufort.

PUT-IN: There's a boat ramp in Sea Level not far from the end of US-70. From Beaufort, drive N on US-70 25 miles to a junction with NC-12. Bear R on US-70 and go 1.6 miles to Cedar Creek Rd. Turn R and go 0.2 miles to the boat ramp.

TAKE-OUT: A small launch area is beside the HQ building on Harkers Island. To get there from Beaufort, take US-70 N 10 miles to Harkers Island Rd (SR-1332). Turn R and go 8.7 miles to the end of the road and the launch site.

DAYTRIP: *Core Sound Exploration. This trip is a 20-mile, one-way paddle from Styron Bay, down the back side of S Core Banks, to Harkers Island. 2 cars or a shuttle are necessary. Difficulty rating: 3.*

From the put-in in Sealevel, paddle ESE across Core Sound to the back side of S Core Banks, a distance of 2.5 miles. Turn SW and follow the line of the island, dodging in and out to avoid tidal flats (during low water) and marsh areas. Landings on this side of the island are few, so if you want to get out and explore the island or just have lunch on solid ground, keep a sharp eye out as you paddle. At 6 miles pass Goose Island to the L. Continue another 7.5 miles to Rush Island, due E of Harkers Island. Turn W and paddle 1.5 miles to the take-out on the S side of the island's E end.

WEEKENDER: *Ocean, Cape, Sound. This 40-mile expedition is on open ocean for more than half its length, with an overnight on the beach. 2 cars or a shuttle are necessary. Difficulty rating: 5.*

From the put-in at the boat ramp in Sealevel, paddle out Styron Bay and head due E across Core Sound. Paddle 3.5 miles across the open water to New Drum Inlet at the N end of S Core Banks. Exercise caution passing through, as currents can be strong and unpredictable. Once you pass the breakers turn SW and follow the coastline just beyond the waves. It's 22 miles to the S end of the island at Cape Lookout. Pick a spot to camp somewhere along that length. On the second day, continue SW until you reach Cape Lookout. Two major ocean currents come together here, creating precarious conditions. Paddle around Cape Point and turn NW. At 2.5 miles reach a jetty; another mile beyond is Lookout Bight and sheltered water. Turn E into the bight and then N into Barden Inlet, which runs between the lighthouse and Shackleford Banks. There's a long sandy beach in front of the lighthouse that makes a nice stopping off point, if you want to get off the water and have a look around. Paddle 2 miles to Lighthouse Channel. Turn NW and follow the channel 3 miles to the take-out.

Shackleford Banks

The smallest of the three barrier islands that comprise the national seashore, Shackleford Banks is also the only one that lies on an east-west axis, perpendicular to the prevailing winds. That orientation has made the island a little less inhospitable than its neighbors to the east. As a result, the dunes are more extensive and higher, and the largest area of maritime forest on the national seashore has taken root here. Also on the island is the herd of feral horses that are the remnants and ancestors of animals that previous settlers left behind when they relocated to the mainland. Sometimes you'll see the horses feeding on the marsh grasses out on the sound. When the tide is right, the animals appear to be walking on water.

Although other mammals are uncommon on the island—as they are throughout the national seashore—birds and water fowl are abundant. Several hundred different species have been observed in the area at one time or another. Some are year-round residents, while others pass through during annual migrations along the Atlantic Flyway. Some of the more common species include the

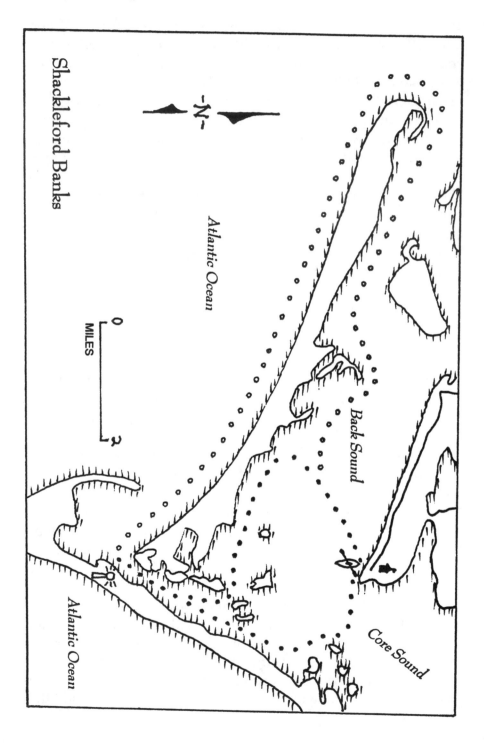

endangered brown pelican, the great blue heron, snowy egret, black duck, snow goose, Canada goose, red-shouldered hawk, laughing gull, herring gull, and royal tern.

From end to end, Shackleford Banks measures 9 miles. On the Atlantic side of the island is a long, pristine sand beach. Behind it are dunes, sand flats covered in clumps of shrub thicket, and then tidal flats and salt-water marsh on the island's sound side. There are no structures on the island, and if you visit, chances are good that you'll have the place just about all to yourself.

MAPS: NOAA chart 11545; USGS Harker's Island, Beaufort.

HAZARDS: Boat traffic is common in the major channels and can get quite heavy in Beaufort Inlet, where fishing boats and commercial vessels heading to Morehead City are abundant. The currents there can be difficult to manage.

BASE CAMP: Primitive backcountry camping is permitted anywhere on the island. If you'd rather not camp, you'll find plenty of accommodations in Beaufort. Tourism is a big part of the local economy, and there's a good supply of B&Bs and hotels in town. Other hostelries are available on Bogue Banks.

PUT-IN: There are several mainland accesses for Shackleford Banks. The trips described below start at the launch site next to the national seashore HQ building on Harkers Island. To get there, take US-70 N out of Beaufort and go 10 miles to Harker's Island Rd (SR-1332). Turn R at the large NS sign and go 8.7 miles to the NS HQ and boat launch site. Other launch sites are at Fort Macon SP and at a WRC boat ramp in Beaufort.

TAKE-OUT: Same as the put-in. If you'd rather use a vehicle shuttle and paddle one-way, you can use the beach at Fort Macon SP as a take-out, or the boat ramp in Beaufort.

DAYTRIP: *Back Sound Exploration. This 10-mile loop trip takes in some of the major attractions on the sound side of S Core Banks and*

Shackleford Banks. Difficulty rating: 3.

From the put-in on Harkers Island paddle 2 miles E across Lighthouse Channel to the shallows behind S Core Banks. As you approach the island, turn SW, paddling toward the lighthouse that rises from the flat landscape about 4 miles distant. To reach it you have to paddle through Barden Inlet, a boat channel. As you near the lighthouse, a long sandy stretch of beach offers solid landing. The ferry landing is nearby, and whatever visitors are on the island will probably be in the area. You can get an up-close look at the lighthouse, as well as stop in at the visitor center to check out a few of the exhibits on local history and ecology. A hand water pump is nearby, but it isn't always reliable. Picnic on the sound side of the lighthouse or cross the dunes to the beach and ocean.

After lunch, paddle back up Barden Inlet until you can turn WNW and follow the line of Shackleford Banks. The exact route you take will be determined by the tide and personal preference. However you go, you'll be able to get a close-up look at the islands and hammocks that dot this part of Back Sound. You can weave in and out of these islands and marshy areas, but if you want to land on Shackleford Banks itself, you'll have to pick your spot carefully; most of the sound side is salt marsh and tidal flat. When you've had your fill exploring the region, or the sun is beginning to fade, turn N and head across the open waters of Back Sound. Harkers Island is 2–3 miles away.

WEEKENDER: *Shackleford Banks Circumnavigation. This 23-mile loop trip circles the island with an overnight on the oceanside beach and highlights that include the lighthouse on S Core Banks, outstanding birding opportunities, and a herd of wild horses. Difficulty rating: 4.*

From the put-in on Harkers Island, follow Lighthouse Channel SSE 4.5 mile to the landmark lighthouse. This is a good spot for lunch, with a visitor center/museum at the site, a water pump that sometimes works, and easy access to the Atlantic beach. After lunch, paddle W 0.5 miles across Lookout Bight to Onslow Bay, a slight bend in the Atlantic Ocean coastline on Shackleford Banks. You'll follow the coastline all the way W to Beaufort Inlet,

10 miles away. Make camp toward the W end of the island. Remember to camp above the high-tide line and to make any campfires below it.

Start the 2nd day by paddling around the island to Shackleford Slue. To do this you have to go through Beaufort Inlet, where you can expect heavy boat traffic and strong, difficult currents. (For an abbreviated trip, cross the inlet and take out on the beach at Fort Macon SP; a car shuttle is needed to do this.) Once around the island, turn ESE and follow the shoreline. The small islands and marshes that spill into the sound are excellent sites for observing shorebirds, wading birds, and waterfowl. As you pass Middle Marsh, Harkers Island appears on the L. Continue along Shackleford Banks until you're ready to make the 2–3-mile crossing across Back Sound to the take-out.

Bogue Banks

Bogue Sound ◊ Atlantic Ocean

A popular vacation spot and home to several developments of summer homes, Bogue Banks is the long, narrow barrier island that stretches 25 miles from the mouth of the White Oak River to Beaufort Inlet and Shackleford Banks. The skinny island lies between the Atlantic Ocean and relatively narrow Bogue Sound. Heavily industrialized Morehead City is at the sound's eastern end, as is quaint, tourist-driven Beaufort. On the island itself, Fort Macon State Park anchors the eastern end and the Theodore Roosevelt State Natural Area is closer to the island's middle. Both are well worth a visit, but most of the people who spend any time on Bogue Banks do so at their summer homes. These line the island almost from end to end. Fortunately, most of the development is tastefully done, and doesn't detract too much from the island's natural beauty.

For kayakers visiting the area, Bogue Banks is a mixed blessing. On the one hand access is easy and the east-west orientation of the banks and the relatively sheltered waters of Bogue Sound add up to pleasant paddling conditions at most times of year. On the other hand, the pristine wilderness on the barrier islands that flank Bogue Banks—Shackleford Banks and Bear Island—gives way to development that is never really out of site and boat traffic that's a constant presence. The best way to minimize the impact of these factors is to keep to the island's western end, where development is relatively sparse, and where the marsh habitat behind the island has been left more or less undisturbed. Bogue Sound is shallow, less than 6 feet just about everywhere outside of the main boat channel. It's shallowest at the western end, where it averages less than 2 feet at low tide.

The single trip described below winds through these marshlands. Numerous other trips are possible around Bogue Banks. The long, sandy beach is always inviting, and even though long

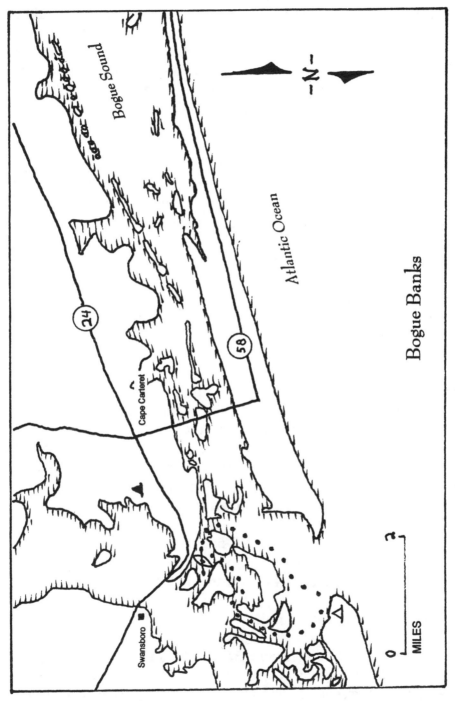

stretches are inaccessible due to private development, public access points are easy to find, including one at Fort Macon State Park, at the island's eastern end. Another possibility is to put in on the sound at Salter Path and explore the natural habitats of the Theodore Roosevelt State Natural Area. For extended stays, you'll find several private campgrounds on Bogue Banks in addition to those listed below.

INFORMATION: Carteret County Tourism Development Bureau, P.O. Box 1406, Morehead City, NC 28557; 800/786-6962. Facilities and services are available in the towns on Bogue Banks or in Cape Carteret of Morehead City on the mainland.

MAPS: NOAA chart 11541; USGS Swansboro.

HAZARDS: Although most areas of Bogue Sound receive at least some boat traffic, the area around Beaufort Inlet and Morehead City are the most congested areas.

BASE CAMP: Since most of Bogue Banks is developed and privately owned, camping options are limited. There's a developed campground on the Croatan NF at Cedar Point opposite the island's W end. To get there: from the jct of NC-24 and NC-58, drive N on NC-58 0.6 miles to the Cedar Point Rec Area entrance, L. A couple of private campgrounds are also on Bogue Banks, as well as a wide selection of hotels, motels, and beach cottages. For info and listings contact the tourism bureau above.

PUT-IN: From the junction of NC-58 and NC-24 in Cape Carteret, drive W on NC-24 2.4 miles to a WRC boat ramp, L. (It's 0.8 miles further W on NC-24 to downtown Swansboro.)

TAKE-OUT: Same as the put-in.

DAYTRIP: *West End of Bogue Banks. An 8-mile exploration of the marsh habitat in a quiet corner of Bogue Banks. Offers a chance to explore natural coastal habitats at the edge of an area of increasing development. Difficulty rating: 2.*

From the put-in paddle E for about a mile, following the route of the Intracoastal Waterway. When the Sky-high bridge across Bogue Sound comes into view, Turn S and paddle along the E side of Dudley Island toward Bogue Inlet, 2 miles away. Dudley Island is a deserted, state-owned landholding. There are stretches of sandy beach where landing is possible. Explore the island a bit and you'll see fire rings left by anglers and hunters who use the island as a basecamp. From the island turn SW and paddle less than a mile to the back side of Bear Island, the major component of Hammocks Beach SP. If you want to extend the trip, it's possible to camp at one of the designated sites on the island (a permit is required). In any case, the uninhabited island offers one of the most attractive beaches in the state—worth a stop for a swim. When you're ready to return retrace your route back to the boat ramp, or navigate a different course through the maze of marsh islands that crowd this part of the coast.

Croatan National Forest

White Oak River

The White Oak River flows out of the swamp forests on the western border of Croatan National Forest. The river begins as a narrow, blackwater creek not unlike many of the other serpentine waterways that lace the coastal lowlands. By the time its waters have reached the Atlantic, however, the river has widened into one of the larger tidal estuaries on the southern North Carolina coast.

Its split personality offers paddlers the chance to explore several distinct habitats without having to paddle great distances. Near its mouth and for almost 10 miles upstream, ecosystems associated with sounds and estuaries are present. Brackish marshes line the shoreline for long stretches, and wading birds and shore birds are commonly seen. Above the small community of Stella, the river narrows considerably and flows through a dense hardwood swamp forest. While year-round residences and summer homes line much of the shore of the lower White Oak, its upper reaches pass through wild, uninhabited backcountry. Here you might see herons, egrets, osprey, white-tailed deer, or even an American alligator. Cottonmouths and several species of rattlesnakes also inhabit the swamp forest.

Although canoeists and anglers in jon boats have long treasured the White Oak River, sea kayakers have not had much of a presence to date. That's unfortunate, since the availability of camping facilities along the river, a low level of boat traffic, and the chance to paddle a body of water that passes through both swamp and estuary areas, combine to make it an ideal destination. And if you spend more than a day in the area, you can combine a paddling trip with an exploration of the Croatan's interior, a 160,000-acre expanse of wetland habitats.

Paddling conditions on the relatively sheltered waters of the White Oak River are typically suitable for all levels of sea

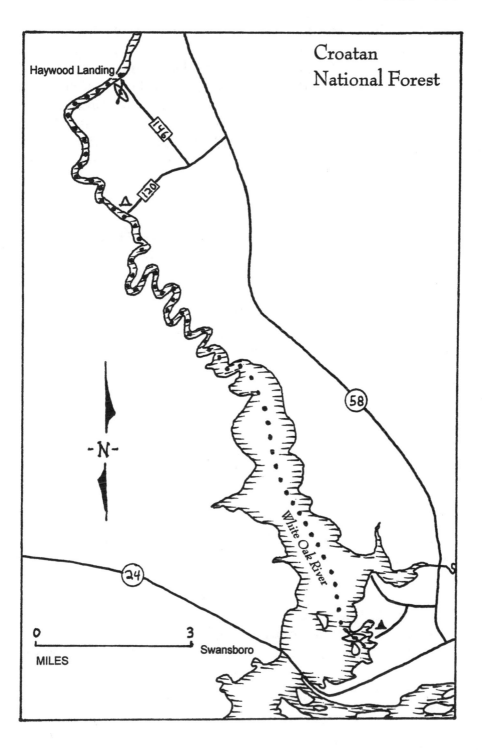

Croatan
National Forest

Haywood Landing

146

120

58

-N-

24

0   3

MILES

Swansboro

White Oak River

kayakers. The river's upper reaches are even more manageable. For longer trips than the one described below, you can paddle out the river's mouth and into Bogue Sound. Here you can explore the marsh habitats behind Bogue Banks or paddle a couple miles southwest to Bear Island, where there are primitive campsites (see separate sections above and below). Several other bodies of water on the Croatan are suitable for paddling trips. These include Great Lake, Brices Creek, and the Neuse River. In addition to paddling, outdoor recreation on the national forest includes fishing, hiking, and mountain biking.

INFORMATION: Croatan National Forest, 141 East Fisher Ave, New Bern, NC 28560; 919/638-5628. The NF information center is located on the opposite side of the Croatan from the White Oak River, not far from the Neuse River. You can pick up maps and brochures inside, and get info on current conditions. Facilities closer to the White Oak River are available at the Cedar Point Recreation Area and in several towns on the river's banks: Swansboro, Cape Carteret, and Maysville.

MAPS: USGS Swansboro, Stella.

HAZARDS: In summer there's a fair amount of boat traffic on the lower part of the river. These are mostly pleasure craft belonging to the people who live along the river's shore.

BASE CAMP: Campers can choose between the developed camp-ground at Cedar Point and Long Point, a small primitive camping area with no facilities beside the White Oak River 10 miles north of its mouth. The former is just off NC-58 less than a mile N of NC-24 and Cape Carteret. It's open May 1 to September 30 and sites cost $15/night. To reach Long Point, follow directions below to Haywood Landing, but instead of turning off FR-120, take it 2.3 miles to its end at the river. There's a small sandy river access here too.

PUT-IN: From the junction of NC-58 and NC-24, go N on NC-58 10.9 miles to FR-120 (7.2 miles S of Maysville). Turn L and go 0.1 mile to FR-157. Turn R and go 1.9 miles to FR-146. Turn R and go 0.3 miles to the boat ramp at Haywood Landing.

TAKE-OUT: From the junction of NC-58 and NC-24 in Cape Carteret, drive N on NC-58 0.6 miles to the Cedar Point Recreation Area, L. A boat ramp is located at the end of the road.

DAYTRIP: *White Oak River Exploration. A 12-mile one-way paddle out of the swamps and onto the open waters of the river's lower section. Highlights are the natural habitats and the chance to observe a diversity of wildlife. Difficulty rating: 2.*

Put-in at the boat ramp on Haywood Landing. Here the White Oak River is a blackwater creek with almost no current. Paddle downstream through the narrow corridor that passes beneath the limbs of a lush wetland forest. The river twists and doubles back on itself several times along the 4-mile stretch before the confluence with Hunter Creek, a drainage of Great Lake in the central Croatan. Here the river begins to widen, to perhaps several hundred feet across. The river's course becomes even less regular than just upstream, with a series of 180° turns. After 3 miles, it transforms into an estuary, with salt water flowing in with the tides. Here the river widens even more, until it becomes more than a mile across as you paddle S. Continue following the river toward its mouth for 5.5 miles until you reach Jones Island and the NC-24 bridge across the river comes into view. Just past the island turn W and paddle into a sheltered bay surrounded by marshland. This is the Cedar Point Rec Area. The boat ramp is visible on the S side of a narrow spit of land.

Note: this trip can be extended into a longer trip or a weekender by simply retracing your route back up the river on the second day. Camping would be at the Cedar Point Rec Area.

Hammocks Beach State Park

Atlantic Ocean ◊ Cow Channel ◊ Bogue Inlet ◊ Bear Inlet

Hammocks Beach State Park seems to have been created with paddlers in mind. The park consists of 2 land holdings: a pristine 892-acre barrier island and a 33-acre tract on the mainland near Swansboro, NC. The island is Bear Island, 3.5 miles long and less than a mile across. The habitats it supports and the forces that continually shape and reshape it are typical of the long string of barrier islands that line the NC coast. A wide sandy beach fronts the Atlantic Ocean for the island's entire length. Behind it, sand piles high in an extensive network of dunes, anchored by sea grasses and thickets of small shrubs. On the island's bay side, small tracts of maritime forest grow in the places most sheltered from the harsh coastal weather; elsewhere salt marsh is cut by narrow estuarine creeks.

Except for a handful of low-impact amenities, the island has been left in its natural state. This benefits the wildlife that relies on the coastal habitats for sustenance. One such species is the endangered loggerhead sea turtle, which comes ashore at night to nest on the island between May and August. The island is such an important sanctuary for these animals that visitors are not allowed on nights when nesting is taking place. Wildlife most likely to be seen by visitors are the dozens of species of shore birds that populate the area or just pass through during annual migrations. These include the majestic great blue heron, snowy egret, and brown pelican. On land, white-tailed deer and grey fox roam the woodlands and shrub thickets. Bottle-nosed dolphins are sometimes seen just offshore.

The island's cultural history is almost as rich as its natural heritage. Native Americans, pirates, Spanish marauders, and Civil War soldiers have all plied the sheltered waters that surround the island at various times. Since the island became a state park in 1964, human impact has been relatively minimal. Today visitors

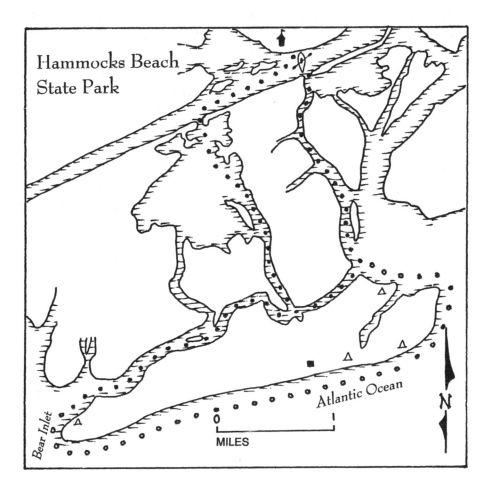

come to swim in the ocean, walk along the beach, camp at one of the primitive beachside sites, or fish for saltwater species such as sea trout, blue fish, and flounder.

With no bridge from the mainland, the island can only be reached by boat. This keeps the number of visitors low and helps preserve the fragile island habitat. A ferry makes the 2.5-mile crossing from the park office on a regular schedule during the warmer months, but kayakers will want to get there by following the blazed water trail that winds through isolated marsh and estuary. Since the park is only one of two in the state that have paddle-in campsites, Hammocks Beach is one of the most popular spots among sea-kayakers along the NC coast. The sheltered water of the marshland behind the island are suitable for all levels of paddling ability, while the surf on the ocean side will test the mettle of advanced paddlers.

INFORMATION: Hammocks Beach State Park, 1572 Hammocks Beach Rd, Swansboro, NC 28584; 910/326-4881. Check in at the park office to pick up maps, reserve a campsite on the island, or check on current conditions. Water, restrooms, and a pay phone are all located there. Water and showers are available on the island at the bathhouse during the summer season; at other times you have to bring your own.

MAPS: NOAA chart 11541; USGS Hubert, Swansboro.

HAZARDS: The Intracoastal Waterway passes behind the island near the mainland, adding to the boat traffic. The inlets at either end of Bear Island are home to strong, unpredictable currents.

BASE CAMP: The primitive boat-in campsites ($5/night) on Bear Island make the best base for a multi-day exploration of the area. The sites fill up on summer weekends and reservations aren't accepted, so be sure to arrive early on Friday if you want to camp on the island. If you'd rather sleep in a bed, check into one of the hotels in Swansboro.

PUT-IN: From downtown Swansboro, take NC-24 W 2 miles to Hammocks Beach Rd (SR-1511). Turn L and go 2.1 miles to the park entrance, R. The boat launch is right beside the parking lot.

TAKE-OUT: Same as the put-in.

DAYTRIP: *Salt Marsh and Barrier Island Exploration. A 10-mile round trip through the marshes behind Bear Island with a landing on the island itself. Highlights are the natural habitats and the chance to get out and explore a pristine barrier island. Difficulty rating: 2.*

From the put-in at the park office, follow the marked canoe-trail 2 miles to the island's W end at Bogue Inlet. The trail passes through a narrow channel in the marshes that form a buffer between Bear Island and the mainland. Here you'll get to observe an estuary habitat up close: salt marsh cord grass, wading birds such as herons and egrets, brown pelicans, river otters, and fiddler crabs. When you reach the island, turn R and enter a wide channel. Follow this 3 miles to the island's E end. At 1.5 miles you'll pass the ferry landing, L, and Cow Channel, R. A wide sandy beach is perfect for landings at Bear Inlet. This is the place to get out and explore or walk around to the ocean side and have a swim. When you're ready to return, paddle back along your route to Cow Channel and the ferry landing. Turn L into the channel and follow the ferry route through the marsh back to the put-in on the mainland. As you near the mainland you'll turn R into the Intracoastal Waterway. Follow that about a mile to the boat ramp and mainland ferry dock.

WEEKENDER: *Bear Island Circumnavigation. A 5–20-mile, largely unstructured two-day trip that winds through the marsh environment behind the island before leading out past the breakers and along the wide sandy beach on the Atlantic Ocean. Difficulty rating: 4.*

The exact route you follow for this trip will depend on which of the island's 14 designated sites you're camping at. Four sites (numbers 11–14) were positioned for easy canoe/kayak access. You can camp at the others, but you'll have to manage a beach landing. Before setting out on your trip, secure a campsite permit in the park office.

Regardless of which site you're camping at, follow the canoe/kayak trail 2 miles from the put-in to the island. The trail passes sites 13 & 14 near its end. To reach any of the other sites you have to paddle between 0.5 and 3 miles. Sites 11 & 12 are recommended, since they're at the other end of the island, 3 miles away. If you'd rather spend more time on the water before making camp, there are plenty of channels to explore in the marshes between the islands and the mainland. You could even paddle a couple miles NE and explore the area around Bogue Banks and the mouth of the White Oak River (see separate sections above).

On day-2 paddle out through one of the inlets onto the Atlantic Ocean. Exercise caution here, as the currents in the inlets are often strong and unpredictable. Paddle past the breakers along the length of the entire island, 3.5 miles. If it's a nice day you might want to surf to shore and spend some time exploring the island. When you reach the end of the island, paddle inshore through the inlet and follow the canoe/kayak trail back to the put-in at the state park office.

Lake Waccamaw State Park

Lake Waccamaw

The third-largest natural freshwater lake in North Carolina, Lake Waccamaw covers just under 9,000 acres. It's the second-largest of the Carolina bay lakes, a series of small, elliptical lakes that dot the Atlantic coastal plain. The word bay to designate these bodies of water is the cause of some confusion: it refers to three species of tree that grow around the lakes' perimeters—loblolly bay, sweet bay, and red bay—not to the lakes themselves. The egg-shaped lake measures approximately 6 miles by 5 miles with a 16-mile shoreline. In addition to its shape, Waccamaw shares features that are common to all of the Carolina bay lakes: shallow tannin-stained water; a NW–SE orientation; a lake bed comprised of peat and sand; and a dense growth of the bog forest type known as *pocosin* around its perimeter.

During the course of the centuries since they first appeared, the bay lakes have been gradually shrinking and filling in. Only a handful still remain as lakes; the rest are simply elliptical depressions that have been covered over by dense vegetation. Although there are nearly half a million Carolina bays between Georgia and New Jersey, their exact origin is unknown. One hypothesis suggests that they were created during a particularly intense meteor shower. Others trace their origin to the effects of wind, subterranean springs, or the erosion of underground minerals.

Lake Waccamaw provides one of the best remaining opportunities to explore the unique habitat of a Carolina bay on a large scale. Although the lake is used by recreational boaters of all stripes, its location in remote Columbus County keeps the crowds to a minimum. A small portion of the lake's long shoreline is dotted with vacation homes; the rest belongs to the lush verdure of the Green Swamp. Conditions on the lake vary, but when the wind is still the waters of the large lake can become mirror

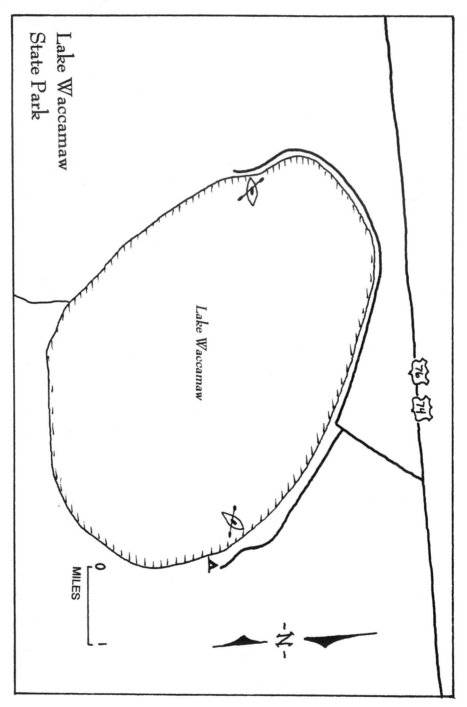

Lake Waccamaw
State Park

Lake Waccamaw

76
74

0
MILES
1

N

smooth. This may be the best time to be on the water, as you can examine the underwater realm from your kayak as you paddle. The lake is not deep—nowhere does it exceed 10 feet, with depths of only a couple feet around the perimeter—making it a good destination for paddlers just starting out or ready to move up to open water without sacrificing at least a measure of security.

Apart from boating, fishing is the most popular activity at Lake Waccamaw. Bass, perch, and catfish are the main catches. The state park covers 1,500 acres on the lake's northern shore. It features a nature trail and a small primitive campground.

INFORMATION: Lake Waccamaw State Park, 1866 State Park Drive, Lake Waccamaw, NC 28450; 910/646-4748. Although there isn't really a park office, a ranger can supply you with maps and brochures about the lake. They also issue permits for the primitive campsites in the park. Restrooms, water, and a pay phone are near the main park parking lot.

MAPS: USGS Lake Waccamaw West, Lake Waccamaw East.

HAZARDS: Pleasure boats and fishing boats are encountered on the lake at all times of year. Although conditions on the lake are usually quite placid, winds can whip the unsheltered lake into very choppy conditions.

BASE CAMP: Camping in the state park is limited to 3 primitive group walk-in sites (the walk is very short). Organized groups can reserve the campsites; otherwise they're on a first-come basis. Lakeside hostelries are limited to a lodge and a B&B. Hotels are available nearby in downtown Whiteville or you can drive half an hour E to Wilmington.

PUT-IN: There are 2 boat ramps on Lake Waccamaw. To reach the one closest to the state park: from Wilmington, take US-74/76 W 34 miles to Old Lake Rd (SR-1740). Turn L and go 0.5 miles to NC-214. Turn L and go 1.1 miles to Jefferson Rd (SR-1757). Turn R and go 1.2 miles to Bella Coola Rd. Turn L and go 1.7 miles to the boat ramp on the R. The park entrance is ahead another 0.8 miles.

TAKE-OUT: Same as the put-in.

DAYTRIP: *Carolina Bay Lake Exploration. A chance to explore the tea-colored waters and lakeshore vegetation of the state's largest Carolina bay lake. Difficulty rating: 2.*

Lake Waccamaw is just about the perfect size for a long day's paddle. With 9,000 acres and 14 miles of shoreline, you can cover almost all of it in a single day. Since the Carolina bay lakes offer one of the most unusual natural environments on the Atlantic Coast, you'll want to explore as many of the lake's various features as possible.

With a profile that forms an almost perfect oval and a shoreline without coves or inlets, Lake Waccamaw requires no planned route. Let the day's conditions and your mood dictate the course you follow. Highlights on the lake are the lush vegetation that blankets much of its shore; the clear, shallow waters that allow you to observe fish and other aquatic life; and the birds and other fauna that make Lake Waccamaw their home.

WEEKENDER: *Extended Lake Waccamaw Exploration. a 2-day, unstructured paddle on the lake with an overnight in the state park campground. Difficulty rating: 2.*

Lake Waccamaw is large enough and its natural habitats fascinating enough to warrant a 2-day visit. You might explore half of the lake one day and the other half the next. Or follow the shoreline closely on one day, focusing on the flora and fauna that ring the lake, and on the second day paddle across the lake's middle, where the sky seems to spread out forever. In either case, the campsites in the state park offer primitive conditions in a beautiful setting just a short walk away from water's edge. And if you tire of paddling, you can explore the coastal habitats on a nature trail, or bring a fly rod and reel and cast for bass in the shallows along the lakeshore.

Masonboro Island Estuarine Reserve

Masonboro Sound ◊ Atlantic Ocean

Wrightsville Beach is one of the most popular sunning and swimming spots on the entire North Carolina coast. The reasons are obvious: miles of gorgeous sand beach, development that is low-key and tasteful compared to many other at-the-beach tourist destinations, and a backyard that includes downtown Wilmington, an attractive waterfront city that combines historical preservation with a vibrant social scene.

Right next door to busy Wrightsville Beach—just the other side of narrow Masonboro Inlet—is a long barrier island that's almost always deserted. This is Masonboro Island, part of the new national estuarine research reserve system. There are two reasons why it's so uncrowded: 1) no development of any kind is permitted; and 2) the only way to get to it is by boat. While these factors may thwart the flocks of would-be sunbathers and swimmers, it's a boon to coastal kayakers who would rather explore untrammelled natural habitats than join the madding crowds.

The 8.5-mile long, 5,000-acre-plus island is fairly typical of the barrier islands that span much of North Carolina's coast, although it is narrower and has lower elevations than some of the larger islands further north. A long, uninterrupted white sand beach runs the length of the island on its ocean side. Most of the rest of the island—almost 90% in fact—is comprised of marsh and mud flats that appear and disappear with the tides. A small dune system also exists and there are pockets of shrub thicket and maritime forest. The island's orientation mirrors the coastline, lying along a northeast–southwest axis. At the island's southern end is Carolina Beach Inlet. Cross it and you're on Carolina Beach, a summer tourist spot almost as busy and popular as Wrightsville Beach. The importance of such a large, unspoiled barrier island between these two heavily developed beach resorts can't be

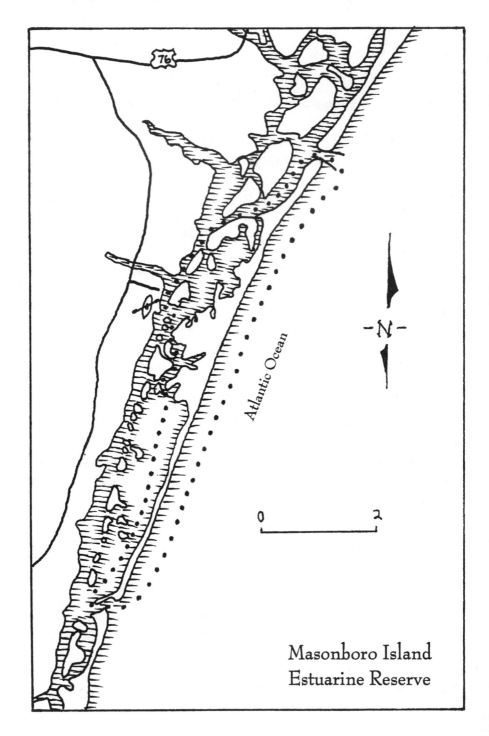

76

Atlantic Ocean

-N-

0   2

Masonboro Island
Estuarine Reserve

exaggerated.

The island ecosystem supports a wide diversity of life. The estuary on the island's back side is an important nursery for dozens of marine species. These include crustaceans, bi-valves, and fish such as flounder, mullet, bluefish, pompano, and spot. The most readily visible wildlife are the 200-plus species of birds that have been counted in the area. Only a few representative species can be listed here: brown pelicans, terns, osprey, black skimmer, and peregrine falcon have all been observed on the island. In summer, endangered loggerhead sea turtles come ashore to nest.

Kayakers can paddle the sheltered waters of narrow Masonboro Sound or venture around to the ocean side and try the more challenging conditions of the Atlantic surf. The sound lies between the pristine island and a mainland that's developed, but unobtrusively so, with scattered homes and the odd marina or two. The sound is on the Intracoastal Waterway, so other boats are a presence, but the setting is still one of the more pleasant on the lower North Carolina coast. Duck behind a large marsh island or beach on a sandy landing and you'll think you're a hundred miles from the nearest barge or commercial development.

INFORMATION: Masonboro Island Estuarine Research Reserve, 7205 Wrightsville Ave, Wilmington, NC 28403; 910/256-3721. There are no facilities at all on the island. Water, rest rooms, and other amenities are all available in Wrightsville Beach and Carolina Beach.

MAPS: NOAA 11541, 11534; USGS Wrightsville Beach, Carolina Beach.

BASE CAMP: Camping isn't allowed on the island. The nearest public campground is at Carolina Beach SP, less than 10 miles S. If you want to sleep in a bed, there are literally thousands of rooms in Wrightsville Beach, Carolina Beach, and Wilmington. The Cape Fear Coast Visitors Bureau (800/222-4757) can supply you with phone numbers and listings.

HAZARDS: Masonboro Sound is part of the Intracoastal Waterway, and therefore sees quite a bit of boat traffic. Masonboro Inlet and Carolina Inlet are particularly busy areas. A long jetty juts out into the ocean at the N end of Masonboro Island. Kayakers wanting to go through the inlet to the ocean side of the island have to go around it. Both inlets are subject to strong, tricky currents.

PUT-IN: From the junction of US-76 and NC-132 E of downtown Wilmington, drive E on US-76 0.2 miles to Pine Grove Dr. Turn R and go 2 miles to Masonboro Loop Rd. Turn R and go 1.8 miles to Trail's End Rd. Turn L and go 0.5 mile to the end of the road and boat ramp. If there's no parking at the ramp, ask if you can park in the marina next door.

TAKE-OUT: Same as the put-in above

DAYTRIP 1: *Masonboro Sound Exploration. A leisurely 10-mile paddle up and down the sheltered waters of Masonboro Sound. The main highlight is the barrier island wilderness of Masonboro Island. Difficulty rating: 2.*
This largely unstructured trip affords a good opportunity to explore the back side of Masonboro Island. You can paddle in and out of the large tracts of salt marsh and observe dozens of species of shore birds. The sound is quite narrow, which keeps conditions on the water pretty tame, even when the wind is up on the island's ocean side. From the put-in, paddle SW toward Carolina Beach Inlet. Your exact route will be determined by tide levels, but keep as close to Masonboro Island as you can, as it offers more interesting scenery than the mainland shore. The distance to the inlet is 5 miles. Between the put-in and there you'll find plenty of sandy landings on the island that invite you to get out and explore, or just take a break and have some lunch.

DAYTRIP 2: *Masonboro Island Circumnavigation. An arduous 18-mile loop around the island, paddling on both sound and sea. Highlights are the chance to observe the flora and fauna of a wilderness barrier island and the long, empty sand beach on the Atlantic ocean side. Difficulty rating: 5.*

From the put-in, paddle SSW toward Carolina Beach Inlet, 5 miles away. Enter the inlet to the L and paddle through to the ocean side of Masonboro Island. From there, it's 8.5 miles NNE along a deserted ribbon of sand. If the conditions are right, this is a great area to practice your surf landings and launches. The isolated setting and strong currents, however, demand caution. When you reach Masonboro Inlet, paddle out around the long jetty and enter the channel. This is a narrow passageway with strong currents and a fair amount of boat traffic. Be careful. Enter the first channel behind the island to the L. Turn SW and paddle 3.5 miles to the put-in/take-out.

Carolina Beach State Park

Cape Fear River ◊ Town Creek ◊ Snows Cut ◊ Masonboro Sound

Carolina Beach State Park is ideally situated for paddlers wanting to explore the major waterways of the southern North Carolina coast. Encompassing 1,773 acres of the northwestern corner of Pleasure Island, the park overlooks the junction of the vast Cape Fear River and Snow's Cut. The latter, a part of the Intracoastal Waterway, was dredged in 1929, creating Pleasure Island and a link between the river and Masonboro Sound. The park sits on the Cape Fear's eastern shore, roughly midway between Wilmington and the river's mouth at the Atlantic Ocean. The attractive riverfront city has been North Carolina's largest sea port since colonial times and has given the Cape Fear River a central commercial and strategic role in the recent history of the North Carolina coast.

Although long stretches of its lower shoreline remain undeveloped, the huge tankers and container ships that travel up and down the river attest to its role as an important commercial artery. Then too, there's the massive, looming bulk of the USS North Carolina, moored on the Cape Fear opposite the Wilmington waterfront. The massive warship, once the pride of the Pacific Fleet, is now a museum and favorite tourist stop. If you paddle the lower Cape Fear, be prepared to share space with some of the largest ocean-going vessels in the world.

Before Wilmington became an important port, before colonial settlement even, the shores of the lower Cape Fear River were home to a tribe of native Americans that share their name with the river. A small band was present when groups of Englishmen from New England and Barbados attempted to settle the area in 1661 and 1663. Their efforts failed, and at least one account attributes their withdrawal from the area to the Indians' hostility. By 1726, however, a settlement with staying power had been established, and the Cape Fear Indians were eventually pushed out of their

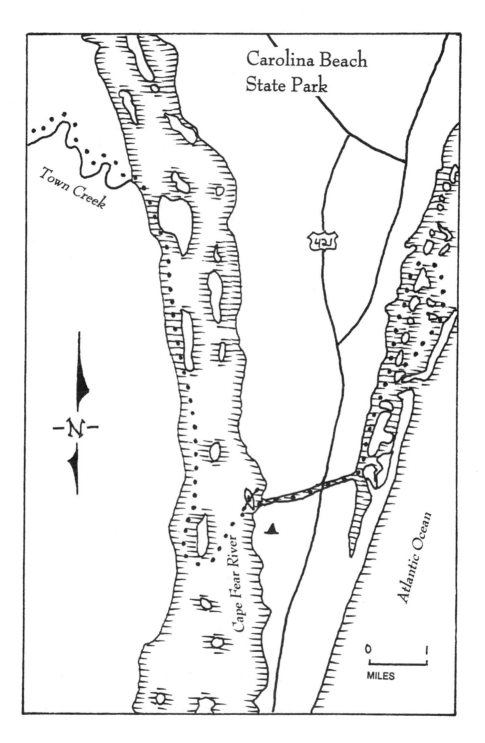

Carolina Beach
State Park

Town Creek

421

-N-

Cape Fear River

Atlantic Ocean

0   1
MILES

home range. The lower Cape Fear River region quickly became the most important port of entry on the North Carolina Coast. During the Civil War it was hotly contested, with Fort Fisher protecting the river and city of Wilmington from Union attack until it was finally overrun just weeks before the war's end. Today Wilmington is the largest city on the North Carolina coast. A revitalized waterfront downtown and the largest designated historical area in the state are main attractions for visitors.

Fortunately, large stretches of the Cape Fear's shoreline are little changed from the days when Indians and British colonists plied its deep waters. The lower Cape Fear is tidal, which affects both current and riparian ecology. Out on the river, you'll pass tidal flats where cordgrass and sedge dominate. At the river's edge are pockets of the lush shrub thickets known as pocosins, an Algonquin word that means "swamp on a hill." Pocosins are home to sweet bay, rose bay, yaupon, loblolly pine, and pond pine, among other species. Also present are at least five different types of carnivorous plants, including bladderworts, sundews, butterworts, and the well-known Venus' fly-trap. These last occur naturally only within a 75-mile radius of Wilmington. Dunes also rise behind the marshy shoreline, including Sugarloaf, a 60-foot dune that has served as a navigational aid at least since the first half of the eighteenth century.

Wildlife along the river is most diverse and abundant in the species of birds present, though mammals, amphibians, and reptiles are also present. Common sightings include brown pelicans, great blue herons, osprey, and egrets. River otters are sometimes seen playing in the river, and the American alligator reaches its northern limit nearby.

With four bodies of water all easily accessible from the state park boat launch, kayakers have plenty of options. Conditions on the different bodies of water vary, from sheltered blackwater creek to the open, often wind-lashed Cape Fear. One advantage of the variety is that you can tailor trips to suit current conditions without having to abandon plans due to weather. And kayakers of all skill levels can find a suitable place to paddle.

In addition to sea kayaking, outdoor recreation in the area

includes fishing, hiking on the park's trails, camping, bird-watching, wind-surfing, and swimming in the ocean.

INFORMATION: Park Superintendent, Carolina Beach State Park, P.O. Box 475, Carolina Beach, NC 28428; 910/458-8206 (office), 910/458-8207 (marina). Water, rest rooms, pay phones, and some marine and fishing supplies are available at the park marina. Other info can be picked up at the park office.

MAPS: NOAA 11537 (daytrip 1), 11534 (daytrip 2); USGS Carolina Beach, Wilmington.

HAZARDS: The lower Cape Fear River is a major shipping channel. Boats of all kinds run up and down the river. Strong winds can lash the river's open water into a choppy froth with little warning.

BASE CAMP: A large, developed car campground (open all year) in the park is ideal as a base for weekend trips. The area is attractively landscaped and provides easy access to the Cape Fear River. Sites cost $9/night. If you'd rather stay in a hotel, motel, or condo, there are dozens to choose from along the Carolina Beach strip. Additional lodging possibilities can be found in Wilmington or nearby Wrightsville Beach.

PUT-IN: From Wilmington, take US-421 S 13.3 mi to Dow Rd. Turn R and go 0.2 mi to the park entrance, R. Follow signs to the marina and boat launch inside the park. There's a $3 launch fee to put in here.

TAKE-OUT: Same as the put-in.

DAYTRIP 1: *River & Creek Estuary. A 15-mile round-trip paddle across and up the Cape Fear River to Town Creek. Highlights are the historic lower Cape Fear and Town Creek, a stillwater tributary that's a breeding ground for the American alligator. Difficulty rating: 3.*
    From the put-in in the state park, paddle out across the river toward the remains of historic Brunswick Town. The crossing is

just over a mile. keep a look out for boats of all kinds as you cross; the lower Cape Fear is a major shipping and boating channel. When you reach the river's west bank, turn N and follow the shoreline. As you paddle up river, a number of large islands appear on the R. These include brackish marsh and woodland and are worth exploring. At 6 miles, after you pass Campbell Island, the largest of these islands, Town Creek soon appears on the L. Enter the creek, but keep in mind that alligators frequent the area. Keep to the middle of the narrow channel and don't do anything to disturb or threaten the animals. The narrow, winding creek begins in the Green Swamp and follows a twisting, turning course for dozens of miles through swamp forest and freshwater marsh. Paddle until you're ready to return. Retrace your route back out to the Cape Fear and paddle back down to the state park marina.

DAYTRIP 2: *Snow's Cut to Myrtle Grove Sound. A 10–20-mile round trip that begins on the Intracoastal Waterway and soon enters the pristine environment behind Masonboro Island, a component of the national estuarine reserve system. Difficulty rating: 2.*

Put in at the state park marina boat ramp. From there, paddle around the harbor entrance to Snow's Cut, not more than 100 feet away. Enter the cut on the right and paddle 2 miles to Myrtle Grove Sound. When you reach the sound, turn N and paddle past Carolina Beach Inlet, 1.5 miles N of Snow's Cut. From here you can explore the numerous coves and marsh islands that lie between Masonboro Island and the mainland. How far up the sound you paddle is strictly a matter of personal preference. There are numerous sandy landings on the back side of Masonboro Island that make ideal spot for lunch stops or to get out and explore the island on foot. In some places over wash is common and getting to the beach is simply a matter of walking across a narrow strip of sand. The island is completely uninhabited and undeveloped. (For more about Masonboro Island, see the separate entry above.) When you're done exploring the sound, paddle back down to Snow's Cut and to the state park boat ramp.

Fort Fisher State Recreation Area

Atlantic Ocean ◊ The Basin

A 4-mile stretch of undeveloped beach provides an oceanfront oasis just south of the commercial strip of Carolina Beach. As you enter the recreation area at the eponymous fort, the deep shade provided by groves of live oaks clues you in that you're leaving the hectic, holiday atmosphere of Carolina Beach behind. Although the proximity of so many hotels, condominiums, and cottages draws inevitable crowds, the Fort Fisher SRA is an admirable compromise between pristine natural habitats and hell-bent-for-pavement development.

Although the long, sandy beach accounts for most of the recreation area's acreage, marshes, tidal flats, shrub thickets, and dunes are also present. 200 additional acres of protected lands at the adjacent Zeke's Island Estuarine Reserve add to these vital coastal habitats. Combined, the areas play host to a wide variety of coastal flora and fauna. Most commonly seen is the vast variety of shorebirds, wading birds, and waterfowl that rely on the rich aquatic habitats for sustenance. Brown pelicans, great blue herons, white ibises, snowy egrets, osprey, curlews, sandpipers, and black ducks are just a few of the species that frequent the area. The endangered loggerhead sea turtle comes ashore to nest during summertime full moons. Atlantic bottlenose dolphins are often seen swimming just off the coast. Humpback and pygmy sperm whales have also been observed among the Atlantic's waves.

In addition to the natural heritage it preserves, the Fort Fisher area is steeped in history. Prior to European settlement, the lower Cape Fear area was home to tribes of Native Americans. The English arrived permanently toward the end of the eighteenth century. Prior to that attempts at establishing a permanent colony had been undertaken by both the English and settlers from the West Indies, but none was successful. It was during the Civil War,

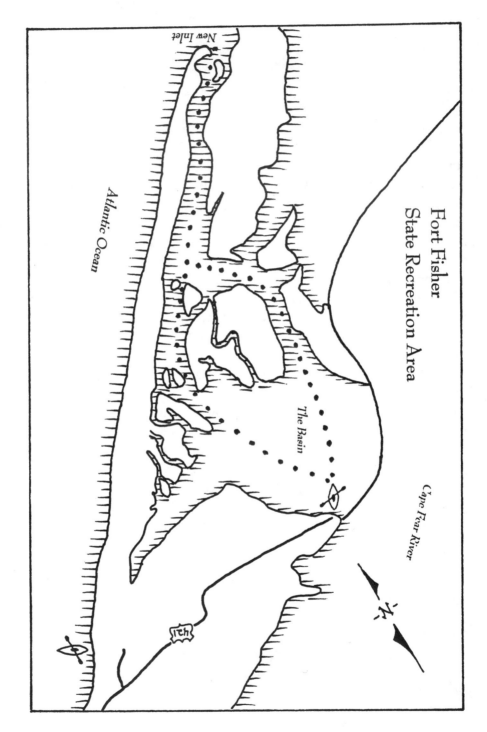

however, that the strategic location of the mouth of the Cape Fear became paramount. Built at the start of the war, Fort Fisher—dubbed the "Gibraltar of the South"—protected the vital port of Wilmington from Union attack. After two unsuccessful attempts on the fort, Union forces finally breached its defenses in 1865. Three months later, the war was over.

Today the fort is operated as a museum and is a destination for tourists seeking more information about the area. A branch of the North Carolina Aquarium is another draw at the site. But the long spit of pristine beach is still the main attraction. Unlike its neighbors to the north, Carolina Beach and Wrightsville Beach, Fort Fisher generally hosts smallish crowds, even during the peak summer season. This is a boon for paddlers, who can follow the beautiful coastline south and then cut into New Inlet and explore the rich estuary that unfolds between the barrier spit and a long jetty that diverts the flow of the Cape Fear River. This area is known as The Basin. There you can paddle shallow waters that are the nursery for an amazing diversity of aquatic life: crustaceans, fish, scallops, and clams are all abundant. Depending on the tides, the water flows over flats and marshes that nurture cordgrass and needlerush and around several small islands. Paddling conditions change drastically here due to the strong winds that often blow in off the ocean. Although the waters of the Basin are sometimes calm, more often than not a wind is blowing.

The Fort Fisher SRA and Zeke's Island Estuarine Research Reserve offer protection for some of the richest and most diverse habitats on the Atlantic Coast. But they also provide ample options for low-impact outdoor recreation. In addition to swimmers and sunbathers, the oceanfront beach is often lined with anglers. On windy days, kayakers may have to share the waters of the Basin with windsurfers, who launch their boards from the small beach next to the boat ramp. And hikers and naturalists can explore the area's ecology by hiking trail.

INFORMATION: Fort Fisher SRA, P.O. Box 475, Carolina Beach, NC 28428; 919/778-6234. Facilities at the SRA can be found at several locations: the fort, the aquarium, and on the boardwalk to the swimming beach. You'll find water, rest rooms, changing rooms, a snack bar, and shower at the latter. A map and brochure of the SRA can be picked up at Carolina Beach SP.

MAPS: NOAA chart 11537; USGS Kure Beach

HAZARDS: High winds are not uncommon in this exposed area near Cape Fear. Water conditions can become quite rough when the wind is up. The jetty known as the Rocks becomes submerged at high tide and presents a real danger. Use a map and keep aware of its location.

BASE CAMP: Camping isn't allowed at the SRA or at the adjacent Zeke's Island Estuarine Research Reserve. This means that you'll have to base your trip off-site. Fortunately, there are plenty of options nearby. If you're camping, head to Carolina Beach SP (see separate entry above), just 5.5 mi N of the fort. If you'd rather sleep in a bed, you have your choice of dozens of hotels, motels, and condominium rentals on the Carolina Beach strip.

PUT-IN: From Wilmington, take US-421 S for 20 miles (at 12.8 miles pass Carolina Beach SP; at 18.6 miles pass the Fort Fisher Rec Area) to the end of the road and a boat ramp at Federal Point. It's also possible to put in on the Cape Fear River from here.

TAKE-OUT: If you make a round-trip, take out where you put in. For a one-way trip, take out at the swimming beach at Fort Fisher. By car, it's 1.4 miles back up US-421 from the put-in. You'll have to portage across the beach, a hike of perhaps 200 yds.

DAYTRIP: *Zeke's Island Estuary. A 5–10-mile paddle that winds through the salt marshes and tidal flats of the area between the Atlantic Ocean and the Cape Fear River. Highlights are the estuary ecology and the chance to observe marine and avian wildlife. Difficulty rating: 3*
Put in at the boat ramp or sandy beach at Federal Point. Paddle S across the Basin 0.75 mile to Zeke's Island. What route you take from here will depend on the level of the tide. Your

primary direction is SSE, navigating through the islands and marshes in whatever channels are available. A good map is essential, and even then you may have to resign yourself to running aground on the flats when the tide is out. At New Inlet, you can paddle out onto the ocean and follow the coastline either N or S. In either direction there are miles of empty sandy beach—perfect for a lunch stop or swimming break, if you feel up to surfing to shore. If you'd prefer an easier trip, stay behind the barrier spit and paddle down to explore Buzzard Bay and the creeks and sloughs that connect it to the Cape Fear River. When you're ready to return, pick a different route through the marsh islands and make your way back to the boat ramp.

South Carolina

South Carolina Key Map

1. Huntington Beach SP
2. Historic Georgetown
3. Tom Yawkey Wildlife Ctr
4. Santee NWR
5. Santee Coastal Reserve
6. Bull Island
7. Cape Romain

8. Charleston
9. Edisto Beach SP
10. ACE Basin NWR
11. Bear Island WMA
12. Hunting Island SP
13. Pinckney Island NWR
14. Savannah NWR

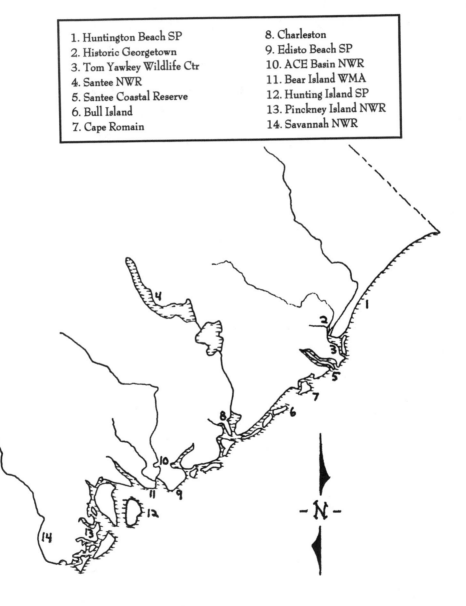

Weather Readings at Charleston, SC

Month	Air Temp (High)	Water Temp	Wind Speed (mph)	Wind Direction
January	59°	49°	9	SW
February	61°	50°	10	NNE
March	68°	56°	10.5	SSW
April	76°	65°	10	SSW
May	83°	73°	9	S
June	87°	80°	8.5	S
July	89°	83°	8	SW
August	89°	83°	7.5	SW
September	85°	80°	8	NNE
October	77°	72°	8	NNE
November	69°	63°	8	N
December	61°	54°	9	NNE

Huntington Beach State Park
Murrells Inlet ◊ Oaks Creek ◊ Atlantic Ocean

Huntington Beach State Park remains a bastion of undeveloped serenity against the encroaching army of vacation rental cottages, high-rise motels, and seasonal businesses collectively known as the Grand Strand—a commercial district that runs from the North Carolina border all the way south to Georgetown. Located just below Murrells Inlet and only sixteen miles south of Myrtle Beach, the park's 2,500 acres occupy a narrow strip of undeveloped coast between US-17 and the Atlantic Ocean.

Formerly the residence of the accomplished sculptress Anna Hyatt Huntington and her husband, Archer Milton Huntington, the area has been set aside as a preserve since the couple bought the land in 1930. Uses for the land prior to their acquisition included rice farming and game hunting. The conservation-minded Huntingtons acquired the property to create a refuge where they could observe area wildlife. Their winter home, Atalaya, remains on the premises and serves as a popular visitor center. The state park system acquired the land in order to continue the Huntington's objective of natural preservation.

For sea kayakers visiting the northern SC coast, the state park presents a rare opportunity in the region to explore a pristine coastal environment. Despite development to the north and south, the park maintains the landscape's integrity with its sparse, unobtrusive facilities. The park preserve allows visitors to imagine how the rest of the Grand Strand must have appeared before the region's popularity as a summertime resort.

The relatively small stretch of land incorporates at least four distinct ecosystems: salt marsh, lagoon, maritime forest, and ocean beach. Predictably these uninhabited wilds support a vast diversity of fauna. Birds find this environment particularly suitable. Great blue herons and snowy white egrets are common

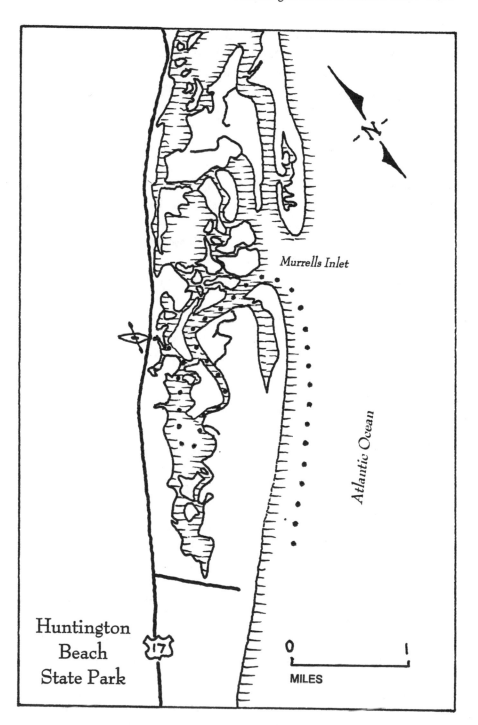

Murrells Inlet

Atlantic Ocean

Huntington
Beach
State Park

17

0   1

MILES

around the marsh. Alligators and ducks inhabit the freshwater lagoon, while deer and smaller mammals thrive in the maritime forest. In addition to the terrestrial species, the waters surrounding the park teem with aquatic life. Murrells Inlet is a magnet for trophy-size fish, and the inland waters provide nutrient-rich breeding waters for future catches.

Kayakers embarking from Huntington Beach State Park have the chance to gain an intimate knowledge of these ecosystems. The major artery of the park's interior waters is Oaks Creek. This so-called creek really owes its existence to the ocean's encroachment onto dry land rather than to freshwater flowing out to sea. Via this conduit, the tide's ebb and flow nourishes the inland marshes. Flanked by acres of cordgrass, Oaks Creek winds its way to Murrells Inlet at the park's northern boundary.

Murrells Inlet marks a rare breach in the almost contiguous northern coastline. The geographic monotony of this region, with few protected bays or inlets, generally forces area paddlers to ply the waters of the open ocean. The exception is Murrells Inlet, which provides a nice diversion for kayakers seeking a protected haven. Unfortunately, larger vessels ferrying to and from the ocean utilize the inlet as well. To accommodate these deep-hulled craft, the Army Corps of Engineers built two enormous jetties to protect the inlet's deep channel. The paved-over top of the southern breakwater provides an extended fishing pier for anglers, but poses a formidable obstacle for kayakers wanting to paddle around to the beachfront. Hardy souls who make the venture are rewarded with an amazing panorama of unspoiled beach—the shoreline south of the inlet is untouched by any development. Dunes covered in sea oats and beach grass line the entire length of the park.

In addition to the excellent sea kayaking, the park offers several land-based activities. Fishing accounts for the most visits year round. The productive waters from the northern sections of the park to Murrells Inlet encourage droves of anglers to test their surf-casting abilities. A boardwalk and observation gazebo are popular among wildlife photographers and bird watchers. Naturalists can enjoy a 2-mile nature trail that meanders through the park's various ecosystems. Sunbathers bask in the sun on the undeveloped beaches. Two beach accesses draw steady crowds from Easter to Labor Day. Across the street from the SP, Brookgreen Gardens displays statues by Anna Milton Huntington in a beautiful natural setting.

INFORMATION: Huntington Beach State Park, Murrells Inlet, SC 29576; 803/237-4440. An on-site park office can provide you with maps, brochures or fill you in on current conditions. Water, rest rooms, and a pay phone are all located in the park, as is a park store that sells a small selection of supplies.

MAPS: NOAA chart 11535; USGS Brookgreen.

HAZARDS: The constant boat traffic near Murrells Inlet poses the most serious danger. Dangerous currents and open-sea conditions prevail at the mouth of the inlet. Conditions tend to be the most treacherous on windy days, but even calm days can be tricky with strong swells.

BASE CAMP: Huntington Beach State Park has 127 ocean-side campsites. The developed campground becomes very busy during the summertime, so arrive early and avoid weekends to assure yourself a site. Campsites cost $20/night. For other accommodations you can browse the scores of hotels and motels that line US-17 and the roads that parallel the shore. For listings and other info, contact the Georgetown Chamber of Commerce (800/777-7705).

PUT-IN: Huntington Beach State Park is located on the E side of US-17 19 miles N of Georgetown and 16 miles S of Myrtle Beach. Although there's no boat ramp, a marsh access used primarily by crabbers and oyster fisherman offers kayakers a convenient place to launch. This put-in is located 1.3 miles N of the main park entrance where you'll find a small gray sign that signals the entrance to the narrow dirt road. If you embark at low tide, park well away from the high-water mark.

TAKE-OUT: Same as the put-in.

DAY TRIP: *Murrells Inlet and Beyond. This 12-mile trip takes you through the protected estuaries behind Huntington Beach SP to Murrells Inlet and then to the pristine beach on the ocean side of the park. Difficulty rating: 4.*

From the put-in paddle S 0.5 mile through marsh and mud flat to Oaks Creek, the main channel of this wetland. After entering the creek, paddle N towards Murrells Inlet. This section offers the best opportunity to spot wildlife. The endless acres of marsh grass bordering the creek attract beautiful wading birds. After a mile the creek's course makes a 90° turn E towards the ocean. Here the development on Murrells Inlet's N shore comes into view. Follow the creek's widening course E for another mile to the mouth of the inlet which is sandwiched between two protective jetties. Boat traffic becomes heavier and conditions become rougher at this point. Paddle E along the breakwater and head straight out to sea. (Alternately, if the open water is too rough, you can paddle across the inlet and explore the estuaries to the N). At the end of the jetty angle your kayak toward the beach. You'll notice that the currents change as you go around to the other side of the breakwater. After you get just beyond the breaking surf, parallel the beach for several miles before turning around. The beach makes a nice place to land for lunch if you're up for surfing to shore. Picnic areas are available at the southern and northern beach accesses of the SP. To return to the starting point, retrace your route. You might want to overshoot the put-in to explore the southern reaches of Oak Creek which are particularly favored by birds.

Historic Georgetown
Winyah Bay ◊ Sampit River ◊ Pee Dee River ◊ Waccamaw River

The waterfront area of Georgetown, South Carolina's third oldest city, preserves an old world charm. Despite the industrialization of some parts of the city, the docks along Front Street offer a beautiful backdrop for sea kayaking the harbor. The historic district dates back to colonial times, when the port was named after England's King George II. The regional economy prospered from first the indigo and later the rice trade. Commercial fishing has also long been a mainstay in the local economy. Shrimping trawlers and fishing boats still line up along the wharves behind Front Street. The converted Rice Museum—once a bustling marketplace—is listed in the National Register of Historic Places. Its clock tower rises high above other waterfront buildings. Several area churches date back to the early eighteenth century.

The success of the local economy was originally due to a serendipitous geography. Winyah Bay's deep-water inlet serves as an ideal passageway for ocean-bound vessels ferrying to and from Georgetown. The port is also located at the confluence of four rivers. The Sampit flows in from the west and forms the artery connecting the docks of Georgetown to Winyah Bay. North of the city the Black River flows into the Pee Dee and together they flow into the bay. The Pee Dee, which originates in North Carolina, is one of the longest black-water rivers in the country.

Essentially paralleling the Pee Dee through coastal SC, the Waccamaw empties into Winyah Bay only a couple of miles east of Georgetown. Named after the ancient Waccamaw Indians, the river is lined with a string of former rice plantations. The east shore, Waccamaw Neck, was home to some of the earliest and largest plantations in the South. You can sometimes spy old plantation houses beneath the canopy of live oaks. Many of the plantations were converted to hunting retreats for rich northern-

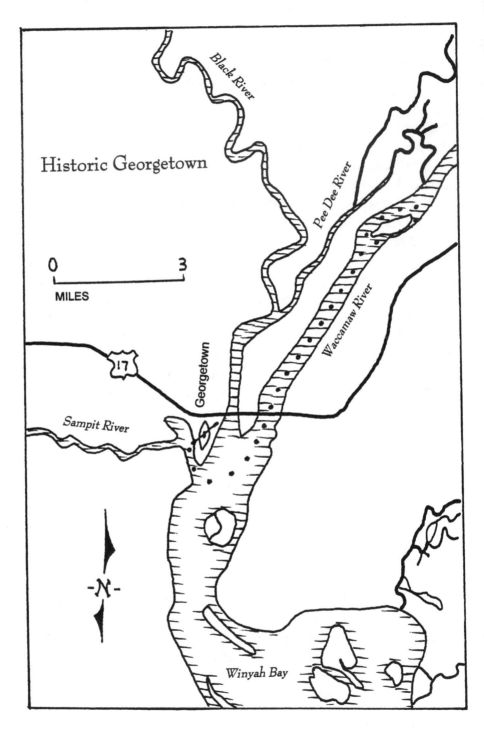

Historic Georgetown

0   3

MILES

Black River

Pee Dee River

Waccamaw River

Georgetown

Sampit River

17

-N-

Winyah Bay

ers during the early twentieth century. The 10,000-acre Vanderbilt Estate is only a short paddle up the river on Waccamaw Neck. Farther upstream, natural areas preserve the river's banks. The Samworth Wildlife Management Area is part of a string of preserves dedicated to the protection of migratory water fowl.

While the water is a great way to explore the historic district and the outer-lying estates of Georgetown, a walking tour of the streets of the historic district is also worthwhile. Just beyond the city, Bellefield plantation has a visitor center and nature based recreation. If you do nothing else, at least try some of the regional cuisine after a long day paddling. The area has some of the best seafood in the state.

INFORMATION: Georgetown Chamber of Commerce, P.O. Box 1776, Georgetown, SC 29442; 800/777-7705. A county park near the put-in has restrooms and water. A small visitor center located on Front St can provide you with information about the region.

MAPS: NOAA chart 11534; USGS Waverly Mills, Georgetown South, North Island.

HAZARDS: The busy Intracoastal Waterway comes down the Waccamaw River and goes through Winyah Bay near Georgetown. Commercial fishing boats as well as pleasure cruisers frequent these waters.

BASE CAMP: The metropolitan areas near historic Georgetown do not offer camping, but the choices for indoor accommodations are endless. Georgetown and the Grand Strand to the north have inns and hotels for all budgets. For more info call the Chamber of Commerce number listed above. Huntington Beach State Park has a developed car campground 20 miles N of Georgetown on US-17. Campsites cost $20.

PUT-IN: From its junction with US-17 in downtown Georgetown, travel E on Front St 1.1 miles to E Bay St. Turn R and go 0.5 miles to the boat ramp at E Bay St Landing.

TAKE-OUT: Same as the put-in.

DAY TRIP: *Rice Plantations of the Old South. This 14-mile trip takes you from the docks of historic Georgetown to former rice plantations along the Waccamaw River. Difficulty: 2.*

From the boat ramp follow the Sampit River 0.5 miles S to Winyah Bay. Turn E and paddle a mile across the bay to Bellefield Plantation. From there, turn N and paddle upstream on the Waccamaw River. The Waccamaw is the easternmost of two rivers (the other is the Pee Dee) that empty into the bay at virtually the same point. Follow the river N 5 miles to Butler Island, located in the middle of the river. Circle the island and retrace your route back to the boat ramp. You should intentionally overshoot the boat ramp so as to take in more of historic Georgetown's harbor.

Tom Yawkey Wildlife Center
Winyah Bay

The Tom Yawkey Wildlife Center encompasses 20,000 acres of managed and native wildlife habitats. The primary function of the preserve is to continue the successful preservation practices instituted by the land's previous proprietor, Tom Yawkey. A well-known philanthropist and former owner of the Boston Red Sox, Yawkey willed the land to the South Carolina Department of Natural Resources in 1976. Resident biologists work at the center to improve his management practices and to learn new ways to enhance wildlife populations.

The refuge sits at a critical juncture along the Atlantic Flyway. Tens of thousand of ducks visit the islands every year. And rare species such as the whistling swan and avocet are sometimes spotted. Predatory birds such as the peregrine falcon and osprey make stop-overs at Yawkey, and two breeding pairs of bald eagles nest at the center. The refuge also hosts many resident birds. One of the country's last remaining pure strains of wild turkey roams the preserve. Red-cockaded woodpeckers inhabit the old-growth pines on Cat Island. In addition to pine forest, the various habitats on the preserve include saltwater marsh, freshwater impoundment, forest clearing, ocean beach, and maritime forest.

These habitats occupy three islands. The largest, Cat Island, has experienced the most land use over the past two centuries. Today wildlife management replaces rice farming as the primary function of the island. Separated from Cat Island by a narrow channel formed by Mosquito Creek, South Island remains more primitive than its neighbor to the north. Center headquarters are located on South Island. Together the 13,000 acres of land form what's known as South Island Plantation, an area that previously existed as part of the mainland. In the 1920s the construction of the Intracoastal waterway's canal isolated these lands.

Across Winyah Bay from South Island Plantation, 6,500-acre

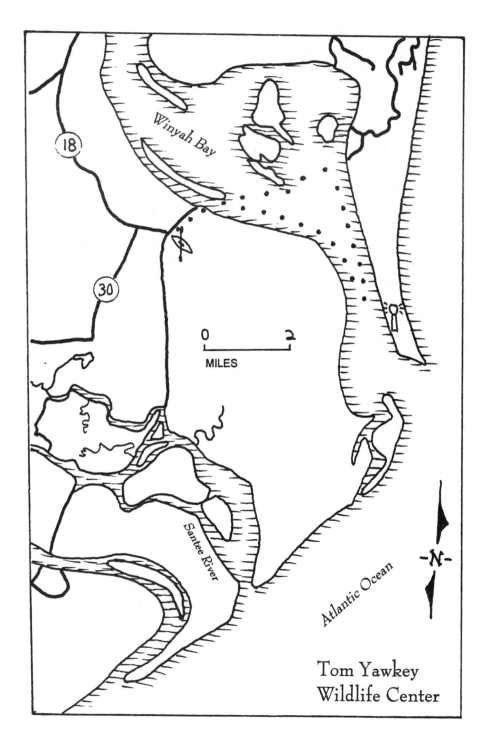

Winyah Bay

18

30

0   2
MILES

Santee River

Atlantic Ocean

-N-

Tom Yawkey
Wildlife Center

North Island is the crown jewel of the Yawkey Wildlife Center. Nine miles of preserved beach extend down the eastern side of the island. On these beaches the dune fields ascend landward for over 200 yards with some dunes peaking at 50 feet. The unusually large dunes present an enigma to coastal geologists—dunes along the SC coast are generally much smaller. These sands create a protective shield for the forest that grows farther inland.

Beyond the dunes, a mature maritime forest harbors stands of live oak, laurel oak, red cedar, red bay, holly, and palmetto. The nutrient-poor sand inhibits the growth of these trees and prevents other constituent maritime species such as magnolia from taking root. The centerpiece of the island, the Georgetown lighthouse has stood at its present location on the west side of North Island for almost 200 years. Several restorations have ensured its designation as the oldest active lighthouse in SC. While visitors are not allowed on the island without special permission from the center, much of the island's beauty can be appreciated from the water.

And there's no absence of water to paddle. Winyah Bay is the largest body of sheltered water on the northern half of the SC coast. It's the first major inlet to breach the coast south of North Carolina. This explains why colonial settlers landed their ships within its protected waters. The Sampit, Pee Dee, and Waccamaw rivers feed the bay from the north. These rivers combine with the vast bay to offer sea kayakers a wealth of paddling opportunities.

Sea kayaking the waters that surround and flow through it is one of the best ways to appreciate the Tom Yawkey Wildlife Center. Land-based recreation is tightly controlled to ensure an unspoiled environment for area wildlife. To view inland habitats you must reserve a ferry ride and tour of the Yawkey Center. These tours happen on one weekday each week and must be booked several months in advance.

INFORMATION: Tom Yawkey Wildlife Center, Route 2, Georgetown, SC 29440; 803/546-6814. While there is an on-site office, visitors are limited to ferry passengers who must book their trips several months in advance. Call the office for more info. Otherwise, the closest facilities are 10 miles away in Georgetown.

MAPS: NOAA chart 11532; USGS North Island, Santee Point, Georgetown South.

HAZARDS: As you approach the mouth of Winyah Bay, currents and tidal forces become dangerously powerful. Large vessels frequently enter and exit the bay. Steer clear of these boats and remain wary of their wakes.

BASE CAMP: Despite the primitive nature of the preserve, camping is not permitted. Santee Coastal Reserve (see separate entry listed below) is within paddling distance of the put-in if you want to overnight in the backcountry. Otherwise the closest camping is at Elmwood Rec Area in Francis Marion National Forest (803/336-3248).

PUT-IN: From Georgetown take US-17 S 2 miles to South Island Rd (SR-18). Turn L and go 8.2 miles to the South Island Ferry public boat landing. The boat ramp is right beside a ferry dock that transports guests to Cat Island.

TAKE-OUT: Same as the put-in.

DAY TRIP: *Georgetown Lighthouse Exploration. This 13-mile trip takes you along the pristine wilds of the Yawkey Wildlife Center and then lets you admire the Georgetown Lighthouse from close range. Difficulty rating: 3.*
From the boat ramp paddle N one mile on the Intracoastal Waterway into Winyah Bay. Follow the shore of Cat Island E for 3 miles. The Georgetown Lighthouse will eventually appear to the S. Bear SSE and paddle 2 miles to the lighthouse. Be wary of larger craft using the main, central channel of the inlet. After arriving at the lighthouse turn N and follow North Island's shoreline for 3 miles to Jones Creek. Turn SW and paddle 3 miles to the entrance of the ICW using the marsh islands as a guide by staying just S of them. Upon reaching the ICW, Turn S and follow the narrow canal a mile back to the boat ramp.

Santee National Wildlife Refuge

Lake Marion

Santee National Wildlife Refuge occupies a string of islands and peninsulas along Lake Marion's north shore. The 110,600-acre lake is the largest inland reservoir found in South Carolina. This impoundment offers the most expansive opportunity for freshwater sea kayaking in the state. The lower midlands' temperate climate makes Lake Marion a hospitable destination year round. The jagged shoreline offers numerous coves and inlets for kayaks to probe. With such a vast expanse of water, the kayaking possibilities are endless.

Santee NWR is an excellent place to begin an exploration of Lake Marion. The natural areas on the refuge provide a beautiful backdrop for paddling. The refuge protects 15,000 acres in the Atlantic coastal plain divided among lake, marsh, and forest environments. Forest types include mixed hardwood, pine-hardwood, and pine plantations. Freshwater marsh serves as a buffer between some forest areas and the open water. Fields are maintained on parts of the refuge. Here, farmers are contracted to plant crops which in turn are used to feed wildlife.

Wildlife on the refuge is abundant. During the winter the refuge serves as a stop-off for approximately 8,000 Canada geese and more than 50,000 ducks. Ducks include mallard, pintail, and teal. Nest boxes are set up for wood duck. Birds of prey often soar overhead. Common species include red-tailed and red-shouldered hawks. Bald eagles have also been seen around the refuge. Deer, bobcat, and raccoon roam the forests. The freshwater marshes produce an ideal environment for alligator.

The common thread that links all of these species is the productive wetland habitat created by the local topography. Lake Marion's enormous breadth of water is a relatively recent addition to the SC landscape. The impoundment was formed by damming the Congaree and Wateree Rivers in the latter half of this century.

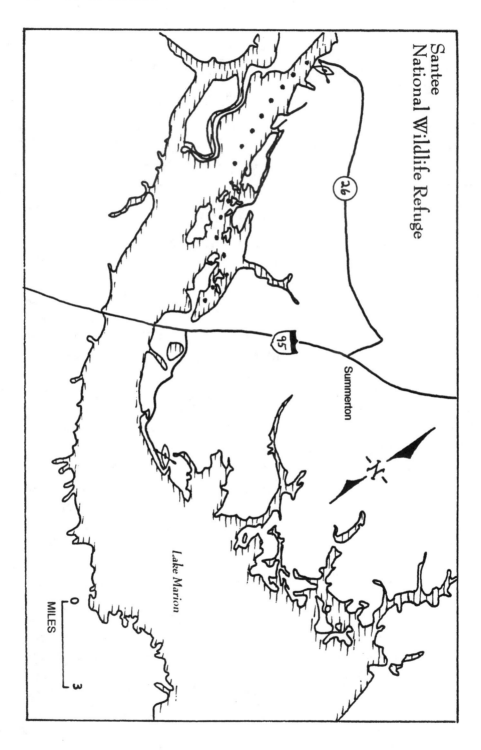

Below the lake the Santee River flows out of the southeast shore to the Atlantic Ocean, and a four mile diversion canal flows out of the south shore to 60,000-acre Lake Moultrie. The Cooper River flows from Lake Moultrie and travels down to Charleston Harbor. Together the two reservoirs are known as the Santee-Cooper Lakes.

The combined acreage of the two lakes is humbling. Kayakers can't resist the wide open waters. The protected areas of Santee NWR and irregular coastline of Lake Marion tend to attract more paddlers than the relatively bland Lake Moultrie. Both offer an inland alternative to the saltwater estuaries of the nearby coast. The freshwater wetlands around Santee NWR present beautiful habitats ideal for exploration.

The refuge and adjacent lake offer other activities beside kayak touring. The most popular activity is fishing. State- and world record fish have been recorded on Lake Marion. The favorite catch is striped bass. The Santee-Cooper lakes are unique landlocked reservoirs for this anadromous fish. Fishing structures are located at a few points around the refuge. A handful of trails traverse the area. A wildlife observation tower along one trail overlooks a popular bird stop-over. A visitor center has displays describing area wildlife. The NWR is a day-use only facility.

INFORMATION: Santee National Wildlife Refuge, Route 2, Box 370, Summerton, SC 29148; 803/478-2217. Refuge officials are available at the visitor center to answer questions and provide a refuge map. The center has restrooms and water. It's located W of I-95 at exit 102.

MAPS: USGS Saint Paul, Summerton, Jordan, Eutawville, Lone Star.

HAZARDS: Despite its isolation from the coast, Lake Marion sometimes acts like a large sea when heavy winds blow. Swells and currents associated with these winds can make paddling uncomfortable and sometimes impossible. The lake is extremely popular among bass fisherman in power boats. Stay aware of these boats and their wakes.

BASE CAMP: Camping is not permitted on the NWR, but Santee State Park across the lake has developed campsites (803/854-2408). The SP is very popular during peak fishing season. You can find lodging at several points along I-95 near Lake Marion. The lake is an hour's drive from both Columbia and Charleston.

PUT-INS: For daytrip 1: From I-95 take exit 108 (SR-102). Travel W one mile to US-15/301. Turn R and go 0.7 mile to SR-26. Turn L and go 10 miles to SR-51. Turn L and go one mile to the boat ramp.

For daytrip 2: From I-95 take exit 102 (SR-400). Travel E 7 miles to the boat ramp. SR-400 makes a L turn after 0.2 mile. The last 2 mi follow a dirt road.

TAKE-OUT: Same as the put-in for both trips.

DAYTRIP 1: *West Lake Exploration. This 16-mile trip explores the secluded areas of the Bluff Unit of the NWR. Highlights are the remote location and the chance to observe freshwater wetlands flora and fauna. Difficulty rating: 2*

From the put-in paddle S 4 miles until you see a cluster of islands on your L. Paddle 2 miles SE through the islands (excellent places to spot wildlife) to Cantey Bay. The bay is a nice, remote region to explore within the NWR. (Cantey Bay is closed to boats from November to February to protect the habitat for migrating birds). The western refuge has a visitor center and other developed facilities if you want to land on its peninsula. The Ft Watson historic site and Indian mound are located here. As you approach I-95 after another 2 miles of paddling E through the bay turn around and return to the trip's starting point.

DAYTRIP 2: *East Lake Exploration. This unstructured trip explores the largest expanse of the refuge around the Pine Island and Cuddo Units. Difficulty rating: 2.*

From the put-in travel E away from the highway to the undeveloped parcels of refuge along the shore. Continue E a couple miles across the mouth of Taw Caw Creek to Black Bottom

Bay. During the warm spring months you might see an alligator out in the open sunning. These reptiles love the freshwater marshes which border the lake. Paddling 5 miles E of the put-in, you'll encounter the Plantation Islands which are the easternmost extent of the refuge This area offers an exciting array of birds to observe. A popular visitor at the Santee NWR is the bald eagle which can sometimes be spotted soaring high above the lake looking to snare a meal.

Santee Coastal Reserve
North Santee River ◊ South Santee River ◊ Santee Bay

The Santee Coastal Reserve's main purpose is to protect the resident and migratory waterfowl that use its wetlands. Refuge lands embrace the North and South Santee Rivers and adjacent wetlands, natural habitats which support many types of waterfowl. The ecosystems present include pine forest, cypress swamp, savannah, brackish and salt marshes, beach, and mud flat. Birds thrive in the region. Naturalists have identified more than 200 different species. The management area features distinctly southern birds such as the endangered red-cockaded woodpecker, Bachman's sparrow, brown-headed nuthatch, swallow-tailed kite, anhinga, and painted bunting. Many of these birds dwell on the two barrier islands, Cedar Island and Murphy Island, where a boat is the only means of access.

Several separate parcels of land occupying a total of 24,000 acres comprise the reserve. The protected estuaries offer a sharp contrast to the development to the north. The reserve combines with Cape Romain National Wildlife Refuge and the Tom Yawkey Wildlife Center to create a vast unspoiled wilderness between Charleston and the Grand Strand. Despite its location between these two heavily populated areas, the reserve does not cater to a large influx of visitors. Only a small portion of the reserve can be reached by foot. Other areas can only be reached by boat. A kayak is the ideal vessel for this means of exploration.

Kayakers can probe deep into the remote regions of the reserve. The ability to backcountry camp on portions of the reserve means trips of virtually any length are possible. The barren tracts of beach front and estuary provide the perfect place to paddle. The sheltered river waters and the open ocean present varying conditions to challenge kayakers of different ability levels.

In addition to kayak touring, the Santee Coastal Reserve offers a few other options for outdoor recreation. A canoe trail meanders

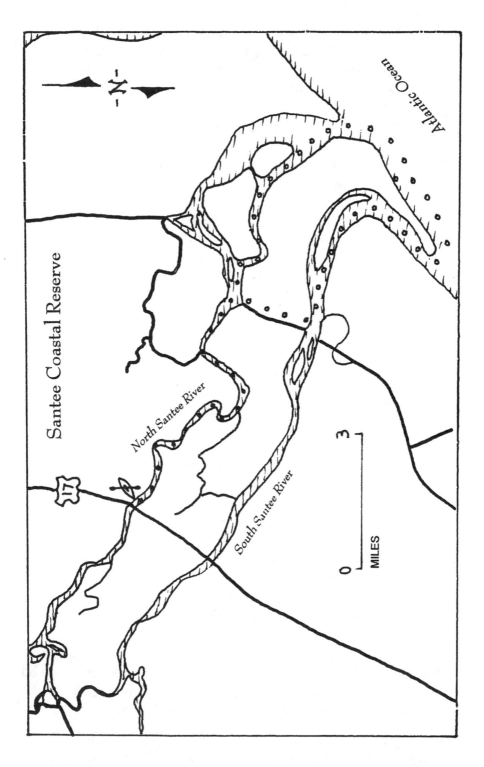

through the waterfowl impoundments. If you tire of paddling, you can hike or bike a 7-mile multi-use trail that traverses the different ecosystems of Murphy Island. This trail provides a good opportunity to spot inland wildlife.

INFORMATION: Santee Coastal Wildlife Management Area, P.O. Box 37, McClellanville, SC 29458; 803/546-8665. There is an on-site headquarters with rest rooms and water. Other amenities are located in nearby McClellanville.

MAPS: NOAA chart 11532; USGS Minim Island, Santee Point, Cape Romain, East of Cape Romain.

BASE CAMP: Primitive backcountry camping is permitted on Cedar and Murphy Islands from February 1 to October 31. A free permit must be obtained from reserve headquarters. Elmwood campground in Francis Marion National Forest is located 4 miles across US-17 from the Santee Coastal Reserve. Other accommodations are available in Georgetown, 12 miles to the north. The Grand Strand offers plenty of motels and rental properties on the coast beyond Georgetown. Listings and regional info are available from the Georgetown Chamber of Commerce (803/546-8437).

PUT-IN: From Georgetown take US-17 S for 12 miles to the N side of the North Santee River. Turn L and go to the put-in. To get to WMA headquarters go 4 miles further on US-17 to SR-857. Turn L and go 1.4 miles to the WMA entrance.

TAKE-OUT: Same as the put-in.

DAYTRIP: *North Santee River Run.* *This 10–20 mile unstructured round trip explores the river's tidal environment several miles upstream from its mouth. Difficulty rating: 2.*

From the put-in travel SE down the winding North Santee River for 5 to 10 miles. Try to time the trip to coincide with the ebb tide for your departure and the rising tide for your return. Take your time and enjoy the acres of marsh along this languid river.

The North Santee River represents a classic tidal environment. If you're at all interested in bird watching then be sure to bring binoculars. This stretch of the river near the put-in has several small feeder creeks that probe deep into the marsh environment. When you have travelled half the distance that you want to for the day, reverse your course and paddle back upstream along the same route.

WEEKENDER: *River to Sea Circuit. This 30-mile trip takes you on both branches of the Santee River and lands you on the pristine coast at the river's delta. Highlights include the environments of a tidal river and the Atlantic coast, as well as the chance to overnight on a remote barrier island. Difficulty rating: 4.*

On day 1 travel SE downstream from the put-in for 11 miles on the North Santee River to the mouth of Santee Bay. Here you can take time to explore the bay. You might spot a dolphin or two here breaking the water's surface. Shore birds are abundant as well. When you are ready to make camp, paddle through the narrow inlet that leads from the bay to the Atlantic Ocean. Travel S along Cedar Island and land at a desirable camping location.

On day 2 continue to paddle SE along the beach of Cedar Island. When you reach the mouth of the South Santee River (The Cedar Island beachfront totals 4 miles), turn R into the river. Travel up this branch of the Santee for 5 miles until its intersection with the Intracoastal Waterway. Travel N 2 miles on this narrow passageway back to the North Santee River. Travel 7 miles WNW back to the put-in.

Cape Romain National Wildlife Refuge
Bulls Bay ◊ Seewee Bay ◊ Cape Romain Harbor ◊ Atlantic Ocean

Cape Romain National Wildlife Refuge encompasses 64,000 acres of preserved coastal landscape interlaced with an intricate network of creeks, bays, and marsh areas that offer an ideal setting for sea kayakers. Ironically, this virgin coastal preserve is sandwiched between two of South Carolina's largest seaports, Charleston and Georgetown. Cape Romain NWR offers kayakers 22 miles of coastline that are a peaceful alternative to the busy waters surrounding these ports. The undisturbed preserve probably looks similar to the landscape that early explorers encountered when they first visited this part of the Atlantic coast—no artificial structures to alter erosion's natural effects and no dredging to create deeper channels for commercial boats. Instead the Cape and its surrounding waters have been largely left alone since the refuge's establishment in 1932, so that the primary forces altering the refuge's profile come from nature.

South Carolina's only cape, Cape Romain juts out into the Atlantic at approximately the midway point of the SC coast. Tides, winds, storms, and ocean currents all assisted in creating and shaping this geological feature. These forces continue to contribute to the reshaping of the cape and its interior islands. The elbow of the cape marks an angular shift in the coastline of SC. South of Cape Romain the shore rotates to a slightly more E–W direction than north of it. A noticeable change in topography accompanies this shift. Whereas north of the cape the beaches stretch out in one long strand of essentially continuous seashore, south of the cape the coast fragments into a series of disjointed islands. This fragmentation results in an intricate maze of interior waters along the state's southern coast. The network of bays and sounds offers shelter from the capricious swells and currents of the open ocean.

For kayakers this means peaceful havens to paddle. At Cape Romain NWR, Bulls Bay is the largest expanse of sheltered water.

The broad, shallow bay offers sea kayakers the opportunity to paddle without worrying about obstructions or larger boats; deep hulled craft can't navigate Bulls Bay's unpredictable bottom. Experienced shellfisherman and crabbers are the only people who dare manoeuver their motorized craft into these sketchy waters.

Seewee Bay, a smaller body of water, offers another fascinating region to explore. The sandy bottom is often visible beneath the shallows, with some areas of the bay averaging less than a foot in depth. Both bays teem with shellfish. Along the bays' marshes, the ancient Seewee Indians discarded enormous mounds of oyster husks. These piles have resulted in substantial stretches of firm ground amid the marsh's soft muck. Farther north of the two bays, a pair of abandoned lighthouses are sometimes visible above the marsh grass. These beacons indicate the location of Cape Romain Harbor just inside Cape Island. Several creeks flow through the broad expanse of marsh, allowing kayakers to explore all regions of the refuge.

The marine habitats of Cape Romain NWR foster a great diversity of flora and fauna. The refuge's broad expanse incorporates at least five distinct ecosystems: maritime forest, barrier island, salt marsh, tidal bay, and brackish impoundment. The diversity of wildlife reflects this unusually high number of adjacent ecosystems.

The refuge hosts 262 different bird species, which can be observed in the area at various times during the year. Pelicans, terns, gulls, oyster catchers, and other shore birds are commonly encountered. The isolated tract of protruding coastline attracts migratory birds on their annual flights along the Atlantic Flyway. Refuge officials maintain freshwater impoundments to provide food for certain migratory ducks—wild millet, banana water lily, and widgeon grass encourage the ducks to winter on the refuge.

Larger fauna also reside at Cape Romain. Alligators are frequently seen sunning in open areas during the warm spring months. In addition to birds and reptiles, 36 varieties of mammals inhabit the refuge. This great species diversity is due to the untainted coastal environment. Any human intrusions are meant to stimulate wildlife populations. Wildlife managers have employed management techniques, such as relocation of eggs deposited by loggerhead sea turtles and maintenance of fresh water reservoirs for birds, to encourage a large number of returning species.

INFORMATION: Refuge Manager, Cape Romain National Wildlife Refuge, 5801 Hwy 17 N, Awendaw, SC 29429; 803/928-3264. Free area maps and information are available at the refuge headquarters. Pit toilets are located near the put-in. There is no potable water source on the refuge.

MAPS: See below under each of the separate sections.

BASE CAMP: Each of the areas described below features primitive backcountry camping on public lands next to the NWR. Although camping is not permitted on the NWR, the adjacent Francis Marion National Forest offers primitive and developed camping options. Conveniently located on the water, Buck Hall Recreation Area in the Wambaw Ranger District has a developed car campground close to a boat ramp. Hotels, motels, and B&Bs are located in both Charleston and Georgetown.

Bull Island

The most popular destination on Cape Romain NWR is the developed recreational area on 5,000-acre Bull Island, the refuge's third largest island. Bull Island is the result of an ancient barrier reef that gradually evolved into a wooded land mass. It is one of the few areas in the refuge that's not completely covered by marsh. Conspicuous from sea because of its prominent forest, Bull Island was often the first land encountered by sailors visiting the SC coast. Stephen Bull, the island's namesake, first arrived here in 1670. The island's relatively large size harbors several different coastal ecosystems, including the refuge's only stand of maritime forest. Live oaks, pines, palmettos, and magnolias all inhabit this

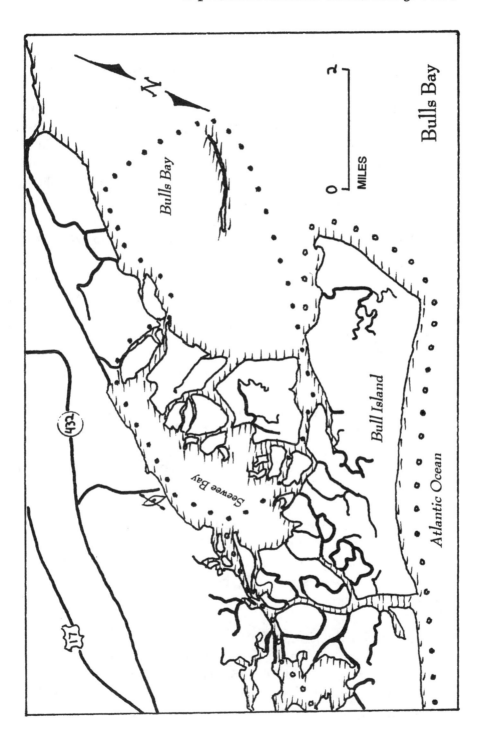

island—unfortunately, much of the old-growth forest was razed by Hurricane Hugo in 1989.

The island makes the perfect stopover during a day's paddle; its firm ground is a welcome respite after a 3-mile paddle. The route to the island is very scenic. It passes across shallow oyster bays and through acres of salt marsh. Wading birds flock to these abundant feeding waters. Once you arrive at Bull Island, the land offers plenty to explore on foot. Despite a ferry that runs to the island, it remains very secluded. You might bring walking shoes to hike some of the 16 miles of footpaths which wind through this maritime forest. The trails include a 2-mile National Recreation Trail that offers up-close inspection of the different aspects of the barrier island ecosystem. Boneyard Beach faces the surf on Bull Island's eastern shore. It comprises the longest stretch of undeveloped shore in the state—a place where you'll find miles of dunes covered in sea oats.

Bull Island also offers limited facilities such as picnic tables and pit toilets. Water is not available, however, and must be transported to the island. Access is by boat only—a ferry departs from Moore's Landing regularly from spring until fall. The refuge manager periodically closes certain areas, so if you plan to land anywhere other than Bull Island check with headquarters first.

MAPS: NOAA chart 11531; USGS Seewee Bay, Bull Island, Capers Inlet.

HAZARDS: The ocean waters to the E of Bull Island can get very rough. Boat traffic is concentrated at Moore's Landing and at the ferry landing on Bull Island. A portion of the Intracoastal Waterway also passes through the area, drawing a number of fishing and cruising boats.

BASECAMP: The Heritage Trust Preserve allows backcountry camping on Capers Island. To obtain a permit call the Marine Resources Center at 803/795-6350. For indoor accommodations, Charleston and Georgetown have plenty of inns and hotels less than an hour away.

PUT-IN: To get to Moores Landing from Charleston, take US-17 N 22 miles to Doar Rd (SR-432). Turn R and go 0.1 mile to Seewee Rd (SR-584). Turn R and go 3.2 miles to Bull Island Rd (SR-1170). Turn L and go 0.5 mile to the boat ramp. This ramp can only be used 2 hours before or after high tide (unless you're willing to plod through deep mud with your kayak).

TAKE-OUT: The take-out for the daytrip is the same as the put-in.

DAY TRIP: *Bull Island Visit. This 12-mile tour navigates the area's marshes and bays and includes a landing on Bull Island. Difficulty rating: 3.*

Starting at Moore's Landing paddle S for 0.5 miles down the Intracoastal Waterway. When you reach the string of long, narrow islands that separate the ICW from Seewee Bay, choose one of the channels between the islands and continue through to the bay. Once in the bay turn SE and paddle 1 mile to an area of extensive saltwater marsh. Choose one of the channels (all eventually converge) and follow it to Bull Creek. Turn E and paddle to the landing on the island. Total distance from bay to island is between 2 and 3 miles depending on your route. Stopping at the island is highly recommended since some of its better sights are only accessible by foot. When you leave the island, continue NE along Bulls Creek to Bulls Bay, a large body of open water. Paddle 4 miles to Bird Island. Circle the island and head N to the marshes. This is an ideal time to identify some of the 262 species of birds that visit the area. An interesting feature on the north bank is the Seewee Shell Mound, an island formed from sun-bleached oyster shells left by the ancient Seewee Indians. Follow the marshy shore SW to Venning Creek. Paddle 1 mile through the creek to return to Seewee Bay. Paddle SW crossing the thin strip of marsh. Then follow the Intracoastal Waterway back to the put-in.

WEEKENDER: *Marsh, Bay, Ocean Beach. This 26-mile voyage takes you beyond the sheltered confines of the marshes and out across Bulls Bay into the Atlantic Ocean. The trip overnights on the pristine beaches of Capers Island before returning to the launch . Difficulty rating: 4.*

The first day's trip covers 15 miles. Begin by following the day-trip route described above to Bull Island. Following Bull Creek, travel E along Bull Island for 2 miles. The broad protected expanse of Bulls Bay opens up to the N and eventually the Atlantic Ocean appears to the S. Follow Bull Island's shoreline around to the ocean side. Paddle 6 miles on the beach front, first traveling S and then SW. These are some of the most beautiful beaches on the SC coast and are certainly worth surfing to shore. Eventually, Price Creek breaches the shoreline. Capers Island awaits on the other side of this inlet. Find a suitable campsite on Capers Island's beach.

On day 2 finish your journey SW along the 3-mile long beach of Capers Island. When you reach Capers Inlet, turn N and go 2 miles to the Intracoastal Waterway. Turn NE and travel 5 miles to Seewee Bay. You might spend some time exploring the estuaries of Mark Bay located halfway between Capers Inlet and Seewee Bay. From the SW corner of Seewee Bay paddle another mile to the put-in at Moores Landing.

Cape Romain

The eastern islands of Cape Romain National Wildlife Refuge, which include the cape itself, offer extensive areas of marsh and tidal flat to explore. The cape juts out eight miles from the mainland into the Atlantic Ocean. Within its interior lies a kayaker's paradise, consisting of thousands of acres of unspoiled coastal environment. Most of this area is marsh, although a few outer islands have firm sand beaches on which landings are possible. Cape Romain Harbor is the largest and deepest body of water in this portion of the refuge. Otherwise a network of creeks and bays snake through the cape's interior. These saltwater channels have no current except for the ebb and flow of the tides.

The still, shallow waters of this wetland oasis teem with aquatic lifeforms and the corresponding complement of terrestrial predators they attract. Areas such as Oyster Bay and Muddy Bay

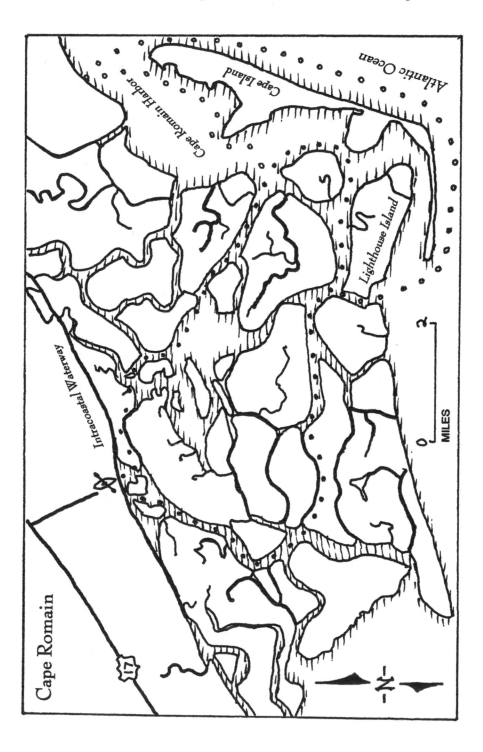

are excellent shellfish breeding waters. Consequently a majority of the Atlantic's oyster-catcher population feeds at the refuge every winter. Many species of fish use these calm backwaters to protect their broods. Fish-hunting birds, including bald eagles, often hover above trying to snare an easy meal. Raccoons are often seen swimming in the creeks from island to island. These resourceful bandits densely populate the refuge; unfortunately they prey on the eggs of endangered loggerhead sea turtles.

Taking advantage of the mobility and surreptitiousness of a kayak, paddlers can get an up-close look at the diverse wildlife. The shallow waters of the area are only navigable by boats with a shallow draft. Unlike Bull Island, this part of the refuge has no access by ferry or other means, so paddlers seeking a peaceful haven should meet with success. By voyaging to the refuge's outer boundaries, kayakers can land on the higher ground of Lighthouse and Cape Islands. These areas offer a nice reprieve from the ubiquitous marshes.

Although isolation in the wild is welcomed by most kayakers, this isolation also carries with it certain risks. The remoteness of many of the eastern sections of the NWR means taking extra precautions. Getting lost in the intricate web of marsh channels poses a real danger. A compass and large-scale map are musts. You should carry as much water as possible, since no developed facilities exist after leaving the boat ramp. Even though sun exposure is always a danger, the lack of any natural cover for miles makes having ample clothing and sun block even more important.

MAPS: NOAA chart 11531, USGS McClellanville, Cape Romain, Awendaw.

HAZARDS: The ocean waters around the cape's point get very rough. The area's geography magnifies common open sea dangers such as swells and currents. A portion of the Intracoastal Waterway also passes close to the put-in, drawing a number of fishing and cruising boats.

BASE CAMP: The South Carolina Department of Natural Resources allows backcountry camping on Murphy Island. To obtain a free permit call the Santee Coastal Reserve at 803/546-8665. For indoor accommodations, Charleston and Georgetown have plenty of inns and hotels less than an hour away.

PUT-IN: From Charleston take US-17 N 38 miles (or from Georgetown take US-17 S 23 miles) to Pinckney Rd (SR-9). Turn R and go 1.4 miles to the parking area on the R. The boat ramp shares a parking lot with McClellanville Town Hall.

TAKE-OUT: Same as the put-in.

DAYTRIP: *Lighthouse Island Exploration. This 20-mile loop trip takes you straight out from McClellanville to Cape Romain, the easternmost extent of the NWR. Difficulty rating: 3*

Allow yourself plenty of time for this long and remote trip. From the boat ramp on Jeremy Creek, paddle S a short distance to the Intracoastal Waterway. Turn E and paddle 0.25 miles until the marsh opens up on the R. Turn S and travel through the cluster of marsh islands until you dead-end into a broad marsh. Turn E and follow its border for 2 miles to the opening of Muddy Bay. A radio tower on one of the bay's adjacent islands serves as a guide. Turn S and paddle across the eastern edge of the bay 1 mile to Horse Head Creek. Follow the creek 2 miles into Cape Romain Harbor and continue another mile E to Cape Island. Turn S and go 2 miles through the passage to Lighthouse Island. The island's sandy beach offers a good landing. From this island follow the Romain River 2 miles W until a creek appears on the L. Follow Santee Path Creek 1.5 miles into Five Fathom Creek. Follow this major artery N 4 miles back to the boat ramp.

WEEKENDER: *Voyage to the Cape's Point. This 32-mile trip takes you past abandoned lighthouses to the outer reaches of the NWR, with an overnight camping on Murphy Island. The second day includes a breathtaking voyage around the tip of the cape. Difficulty rating: 5.*

On day 1 follow the daytrip route to Cape Island. Instead of travelling S to Lighthouse Island, paddle N to Cape Romain Harbor. Follow Cape Island's irregular shoreline which extends NE along the harbor. Use its shoreline to guide you 4 miles through the mouth of the harbor. Murphy Island is the landmass due N as you exit into the Atlantic Ocean. Land along its shores to find a campsite.

On day 2 paddle S a mile across the Cape Romain harbor using the northern edge of Cape Island as a guide. When you reach Cape Island, follow its oceanside shoreline S for 5 miles to the point of the cape. (If you're not comfortable paddling on the open ocean, you can follow a return route back through the protected estuaries behind the cape). The sandy eastern shores of Cape Island make nice places to land before travelling back through the marshes. After paddling around the point, paddle due W 2 miles to the end of the island. From there paddle N a mile to Lighthouse Island. Follow its shore W around to an inlet which leads to the Romain River. Turn W and follow the Romain River 2 miles until a creek appears on the L. Follow Santee Path Creek 1.5 miles into Five Fathom Creek. Follow this major artery N 4 miles back to the boat ramp.

Charleston

Charleston Harbor ◊ Ashley River ◊ Cooper River

The largest seaport in South Carolina and one of the major seaports on the Atlantic coast, Charleston gives visitors a different perspective of the SC coastal region. Wilderness areas have long been overrun in this historic city, and contemporary high-rise development evolved too late to take hold. Instead, visitors see a traditional seaport that grew up just a few miles from the Atlantic Ocean. Well-protected from the surf that crashes on the outer beaches, the tiny peninsula of Charleston juts out into Charleston Harbor. This protected bay sits peacefully inside the natural barriers of Sullivans and James Islands. Here the calm waters attract a diversity of water craft. Large sailing vessels and wind surfers take advantage of regular winds. Commercial freighters land at the numerous inland docks. Navy ships enter and exit the bay on maneuvers. All contribute to the character of the harbor. Charleston and its surrounding waters are not places to find solitude, but they make up for what they lack in serenity with cultural richness and historical charm.

While paddlers can't nearly experience all of this charm from the water, travelling by kayak gives adventurers a perspective of Charleston that early seafarers must have seen—a protected finger of land located at the confluence of two major rivers and conveniently close to the Atlantic Ocean. This perfect geographical location accounts for the early settlement and continued usefulness of the seaport. Seventeenth century seafarers found a safe haven for their ships at the area's first settlement, Charles Towne Landing, located on the Ashley river's west bank. Occupied today by a state park, the landing has been restored in a fashion similar to the former colonial settlement. A replica of a seventeenth-century trading ship and a natural habitat zoo with animals present during colonial times give visitors a sense of early Charleston.

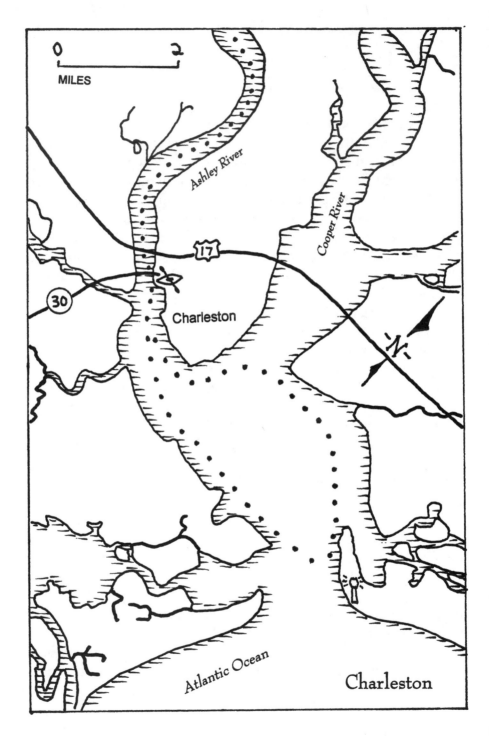

MILES

Ashley River

Cooper River

17

30

Charleston

N

Atlantic Ocean

Charleston

When the city spread east, the region grew as an economic center as well as a military stronghold. Shipping docks began to spring up along both the Ashley and Cooper rivers. The strategic importance of the area resulted in several military installations during the eighteenth and nineteenth centuries. Area forts played prominent roles in both American wars. Charleston became the gateway to the southeast, with travelers entering from the north and abroad to begin journeys to points south.

Today the busy port combines function with elegance. The historical appeal has a well-preserved and -documented presence. Tourism joins the shipping business and the military as a top sector in the local economy. The scenic highlights are endless. A trip to the mouth of Charleston Harbor reveals the strategic significance of Fort Sumter—the site where the first shots were fired in the Civil War. On Sullivans Island another retired fort, Fort Moultrie, played a pivotal role in the Revolutionary War. At the battery on Charleston's south shore, centuries-old houses stand only yards from the water. The buildings never exceed a few stories, giving the area an old-world charm. Palmetto, the state tree, and live oak add greenery at White Point Gardens at the tip of the battery. Farther up the Ashley River, magnolias, azaleas, and camellias give the landscape vibrant colors during the early months of the year. The mixture of natural and historical features provides a beautiful backdrop for a lazy day spent paddling the waters around the city. Not only does kayaking offer a more distinctive perspective of the city than conventional touring, but it also allows you to see more sites in a day than you would by any other means.

First-time visitors to Charleston should certainly stay at one of the many local inns or hotels in order to absorb the unique atmosphere that permeates the city. Attractions other than water-based recreation are abundant. Gardens, museums, historical sites, and antique shopping lead most people's lists of things to do. The city also hosts many large-scale events during the year such as the Spoleto and Wildlife Festivals. During the warmer months Charleston Harbor becomes the major attraction. While enjoying a day out paddling you'll likely encounter fellow kayakers. You can also expect to encounter many other types of craft, including magnificent sailing vessels and giant chartered tour boats.

INFORMATION: Charleston Visitor Center, 375 Meeting St., Charleston, SC 29401; 800/868-8118. The visitor center can provide you with a wealth of information on the city, from attractions to tours to listings of accommodations.

MAPS: NOAA chart 11524; USGS Charleston, Johns Island James Island, Fort Moultrie.

HAZARDS: Despite being an inland body of water, Charleston Harbor sometimes behaves like an unruly sea, becoming choppy and rough when heavy winds blow. The harbor serves as the passageway for large ships, especially along the Cooper River.

BASE CAMP: No camping areas are located near the city, but many inns and hotels are located in downtown Charleston. In addition, area beaches such as Folly Beach, Sullivans Island, Kiawah Island, Seabrook Island, and Isle of Palms have numerous rental cottages.

PUT-INS: For daytrip 1: the Charleston City Marina is located on Lockwood Drive in downtown Charleston. The entrance is 0.5 mile S of the junction between Lockwood Drive and US-17. A $5 usage permit is required to access the boat ramp. You can obtain the permit from inside the marina during business hours.

For daytrip 2: Follow SC-642 N 14 miles from its junction with I-26 in North Charleston to SR-373 (the road leading to Old Dorchester State Park). Turn L and drive to a boat ramp located E of the park entrance.

TAKE-OUT: For both daytrips, the take-out is the same as the put-in for daytrip 1 (Charleston City Marina).

DAYTRIP 1: *Historic Charleston Waterfront. This trip takes you on a 16-mile tour of the historic sites around Charleston Harbor. In addition*

to the monuments you'll likely spy dolphin romping around the harbor.
Difficulty rating: 3.

From the marina head S on the Ashley river. You'll travel a mile before the river empties into the harbor. Bear SE toward the mouth of the harbor using Fort Sumter as a reference point. Go 3 miles to the Fort. After a tour of the landmark, paddle E a mile to Fort Moultrie. You'll notice a lighthouse nearby. The beach in front of the fort makes a nice landing. On your return trip aim for Castle Pinckney Monument on Shutes Folly Island E of the Charleston peninsula. During this 3-mile leg of the trip you'll likely encounter one of the many giant container ships that ferry to and from the harbor. The battery sits 0.5 mile due W from the monument. Many of the houses along the battery date back to the seventeenth and eighteenth centuries. Follow the shoreline 2 miles around to the W side of the battery. Paddle up the W side of the Charleston peninsula to Charles Towne Landing 3 miles upstream on the Ashley River. Here you'll find the replica of a colonial trading vessel, the Adventure, on a feeder creek to the river. Return S down the Ashley River to the put-in, where you'll find the boat ramp behind the numerous moored sailboats.

DAYTRIP 2: *Upper Reaches of the Ashley. This 22-mile trip takes you down the magnificently lush banks of the upper Ashley River. The one-way trip requires two cars and a full day. Difficulty rating: 2.*

While in the Charleston area, you might want to mingle the city's civilized charm with some of the rustic treasures several miles upstream on the Ashley River. From the put-in at Old Dorchester SP, you'll paddle S for 18 miles on the slow-moving blackwater river until it empties into Charleston Harbor. Tremendous live oaks draped in spanish moss shade your journey. Old plantations and gardens color the river's banks. Places such as Drayton Hall, Magnolia Gardens, and Millbrook Plantation line the Ashley. The area is particularly beautiful in the early part of the year when its flowers come into full bloom. Near the end of your journey, Charles Towne Landing is a nice diversion on the W bank before taking out at the City Marina on Charleston peninsula.

Edisto Beach State Park

Big Bay Creek ◊ Scott Creek ◊ South Edisto River ◊ Atlantic Ocean

With all the undisturbed coastal regions on the southern coast of South Carolina, paddlers might dismiss Edisto Island as a commercial beach with little to offer hardcore adventurers. But this analysis severely shortchanges the island's split personality. While a large percentage of the beachfront is blanketed with seasonal businesses and vacation rental properties, other sections of the island maintain a well-preserved archaeological and natural heritage. Edisto Beach State Park plays a vital role in this preservation. Its 1,255 acres include a significant portion of beach and an even more significant expanse of interior wetland. The state park offers kayakers an undeveloped tract of beachfront to admire and remote estuaries to explore.

Edisto Island also holds a rich cultural history. Prior uses for the island have ranged from Caribbean rum-runner hideaway to Sea Island cotton plantation. Before Western colonization the Edisto Indians thrived in this region. Native American artifacts, embedded throughout the natural areas, document a lost culture on the island. This civilization dates back several thousand years. Artifacts around the park attest to their once flourishing culture. The most notable record of the tribe is Spanish Mount, a man-made shell mound. Dating back to 2,000 B.C., the mysterious work is the second-oldest Native American pottery site in South Carolina. Other similar structures have been discovered along the coasts of Georgia and Florida. The purpose of the mound—a giant shell ring which is filled in the center—remains an enigma.

The Island harbors prehistoric treasures as well. The fossilized fragments of ancient plants and animals often wash up on the island. Exposed specimens date back millions of years. Some of these fossils and petrified remains present evidence of long-gone beasts such as bison, mastodons, and giant armadillos. With the mobility of a kayak, turning up some of these ancient remains

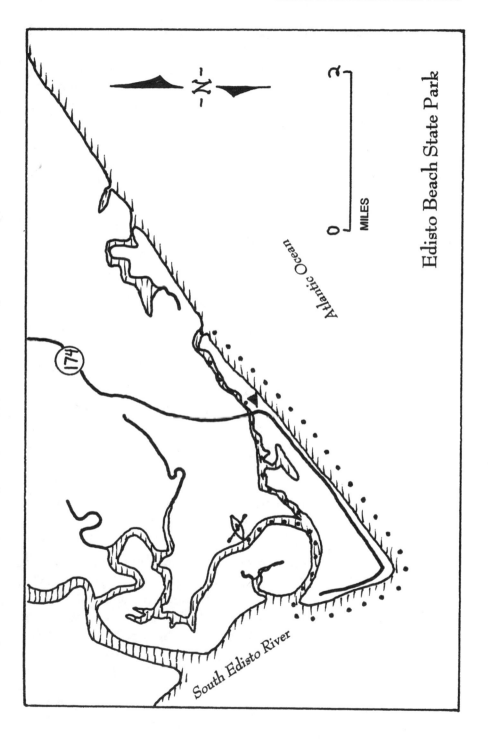

becomes an exciting possibility. (Note: do not remove or disturb any artifacts in the park without permission).

In addition to the archaeological wonders of Edisto Island, a well-preserved natural configuration has also survived time. The vegetation's succession in the eastern park demonstrates a classic coastal environment. A protective barrier of dunes fronts the park's preserved beach. Sea oats and beach grass struggle to stabilize the dunes against the constant winds and eroding shoreline. Only two regional trees, palmetto and live oak, adapted to survive this harsh ocean environment. A dense forest of these trees stands just behind the dunes. The live oak's canopy demonstrates a classic wedge shape formed by the natural pruning of wind and salt spray. Mixed in with the oaks, the tallest palmettos in the state tower above all other vegetation. As the forest extends farther from the sea, pine and sand-tolerant hardwoods begin to appear. Behind the maritime forest a marsh generates nutrients for the food chain's base; Scott Creek alternately feeds and drains the marsh grass with seawater.

A short paddle from ocean to marsh covers this entire ecological cross-section. The respective change in birds from shore to wading species takes place over a short distance from Jeremy Inlet to the heart of Scott Creek. If you go a little further you can observe the contrast between these natural areas with the man-made development to the west.

This combination of preservation and development makes Edisto Island a popular vacation spot. Visitors who enjoy going out into nature and then retreating back to their indoor accommodations find the perfect compromise in Edisto Island. The proximity of rental cottages and hotels to the abundant wildlands gives these vacationers the best of both worlds. More avid outdoorsmen set up camp in the sylvan setting of Edisto Beach State Park. The park features a four-mile nature trail and there are plans to create a primitive camping area. The beach is known for the collection of shells that wash ashore. Beachcombers have uncanny luck tracking their favorite specimens during the falling tide.

INFORMATION: Edisto Beach State Park, 8377 State Cabin Road, Edisto Island, SC 29438; 803/869-2156. The main park entrance is located near the beach on SC-174. At the park office you can retrieve area maps and information. Facilities here include bathhouses, picnic tables, and potable water.

MAPS: NOAA chart 11522; USGS Edisto Island, Edisto Beach.

BASE CAMP: The state park has 103 developed campsites. 75 of these are located on the beach front. 5 vacation cabins on Big Bay Creek are available for rental. Edisto Island also has a plethora of rental properties.

PUT-IN: From the Ashley River bridge in downtown Charleston, take US-17 S 11.5 miles to SC-162. Veer L and go 12 miles to SC-164. Stay straight on SC-164 and go 3 miles to SC-174. Turn L and go 16.6 miles to Palmetto Rd (SR-2352). Turn R and go 1.4 miles to an unmarked dirt road. Veer L and go 0.7 miles to the landing.

TAKE-OUT: Same as the put-in.

DAYTRIP: *Edisto Indian Artifact Expedition. This 11-mile trip takes you on a tour of the former haunts of the ancient Edisto Indians and prohibition-era Caribbean rum-runners. Difficulty rating: 4.*
    After setting out from the boat ramp, paddle S on Big Bay Creek for 0.5 mile until it intersects with Scott Creek. Turn L into the creek. A couple hundred yards beyond the creeks' confluence you will pass Spanish Mount, the ancient Indian shell mound located on the N bank. Follow Scott Creek for 3 miles until it empties into the ocean at Jeremy Inlet. Scott Creek forms the park boundary as well as the county line between Colleton and Charleston counties. The eastern sections of the creek flow through the more remote regions of Edisto Island. If the conditions permit, travel out into the open ocean. Turn W to parallel the front of Edisto Island. The beautiful beach front makes for an ideal landing site. Follow the shoreline 4 miles to the mouth of the South Edisto river. Turn R up the river and paddle a mile to Big

Bay Creek. This creek will take you 2 miles back to the starting point. (Be careful not to end up on Scott Creek again by staying to the L).

ACE Basin
Ashepoo River ◊ Combahee River ◊ S Edisto River ◊ St Helena Sound

The ACE Basin describes a large-scale cooperative project to preserve a major expanse of the South Carolina lowcountry. State and federal agencies, environmental organizations, and private landowners comprise the main inputs into this massive conservation effort which originated in 1990. The Ashepoo, Combahee, and (South) Edisto (A.C.E.) rivers form the major drainages for this fragile environment. The 350,000-acre ACE Basin encompasses extensive stretches of these coastal rivers and their associated wetlands.

The basin represents one of the largest undeveloped wetland ecosystems still surviving on the Atlantic coast. The enormous diversity of wildlife that the region supports, including a number of rare or endangered species, mandated this conservation effort. Sea kayakers possess the ideal vessel from which to witness the birds and other animals that inhabit the wildlands of the ACE Basin. Even though only a small portion of the land has public access, kayakers are able to observe much of the region via the network of rivers, creeks, tidal flats, and bays that wind through the basin's acreage.

Visitors can easily gauge the success of the project by observing the myriad bird species that flourish around the basin. Roaming the calm tidal rivers and creeks armed with a favorite field guide and a pair of binoculars, a kayaker can spot many of the 265 bird species that have been observed in the ACE, or maybe add a new one to the list. The region accounts for forty percent of the state's wading bird population. During a recent breeding season a white ibis colony built almost 12,000 nests. Meanwhile, endangered wood storks continue their reemergence in the basin.

This exceptional diversity of bird species is attributed to the variety of hospitable environments. The habitats include pine plantations, pine-hardwood forest, bottomland hardwoods, managed wetland, maritime forest, estuarine marsh, and beach. At the extreme northwest portion of the ACE, a rare natural stand of long-leaf pine survives. During a single day's paddle, you can observe most, if not all, of these natural communities. Stealthy paddlers often encounter some of the ACE's resident mammals. Otter and mink patrol the upper wetlands, while deer roam the oak forests. The lower stretches of marsh and beach host a diversity of shellfish and crustaceans. The ebb tide encourages raccoons and water birds such as herons, egrets, and ibises to pick through the muck in search of a meal.

In the first couple of centuries of colonial settlement, the region was home to enormous rice plantations. South Carolina's coastal economy depended on these plantations up until the late 1800s. Later, wealthy sportsmen acquired the land to use as game preserves. Fortunately, these hunters were wise stewards of the natural habitats and left them in the largely undisturbed state in which they appear today.

INFORMATION: ACE Basin Project, SCDNR, Route 1, Box 25, Green Pond, SC 29446; 803/844-8957. The ACE Basin is in a remote part of the state where amenities are limited. See below under each of the 2 headings for additional information.

MAPS: see below under the individual headings.

ACE Basin National Wildlife Refuge

The National Wildlife Refuge occupies approximately 12,000 acres in the northwestern section of the ACE Basin. Future plans will push refuge land holdings to near 20,000 acres. The Edisto Unit, the northern of two non-contiguous units, offers water-based access. The area encompasses a beautiful stretch of the South Edisto River where small feeder creeks penetrate deep into the marsh. Jehossee Island constitutes the major land mass among these waters. Marsh comprises most of the island. Refuge wide,

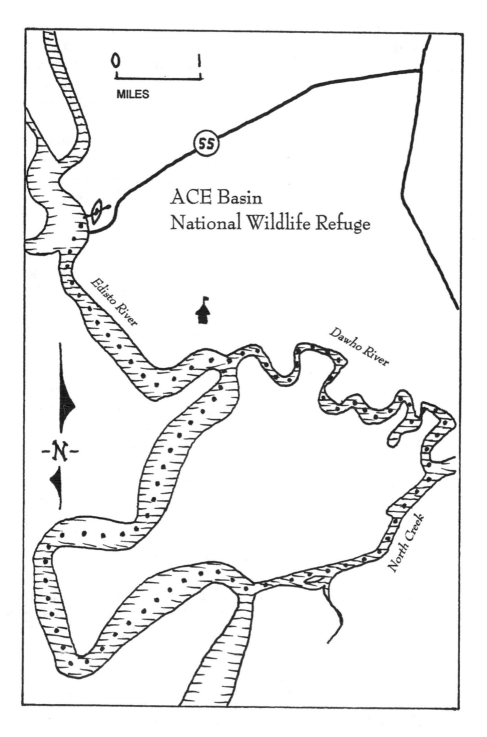

marsh occupies forty percent of the total acreage. The lack of solid ground makes boats the primary means of access to the preserve. While the broad Edisto river hosts a moderate amount of boat traffic, kayakers can escape the wildlife-disturbing whine of motorized craft by keeping to shallower regions. Although refuge personnel are very helpful, the NWR isn't set up to cater to a large influx of visitors. A relatively small number of people make the effort to explore this wild region that has few comforts.

While no facilities exist, the NWR engages in more management practices than do other sections of the ACE. Man-made impoundments provide habitat for endangered species such as wood storks, bald eagles, and alligators, as well as for 17 species of water fowl. Controlled water flow is the primary management technique used to enhance this habitat. The rice fields that once dominated the region were easily transformed into wildlife impoundments. An eighteenth century agricultural tool called a rice field trunk finds a modern-day use in wildlife conservation. These trunks, which are essentially water gates between the impoundments and their surrounding waters, still provide the most efficient means to control tidal water flow. Other important management techniques include selective burning and thinning of trees as well as planting of more desirable species.

Along with the rice fields, the region left behind several former plantation houses. Many still lurk behind centuries-old oaks draped with spanish moss. The refuge headquarters is located in one such house that dates back to 1828—one of three antebellum mansions remaining in the ACE Basin. The boat ramp sits near a community of these houses called Willtown Bluff. Formerly New London, this old south colony was established in 1685.

INFORMATION: Refuge Manager, ACE Basin National Wildlife Refuge, P.O. Box 848, Hollywood, SC 29449; 803/889-3084. Refuge headquarters are located at the end of a dirt road (SR-346) S of SR-55. No facilities exist on the refuge. Managers can offer limited maps and answer questions during business hours: 7:30 AM–4 PM, Mon-Fri.

MAPS: NOAA chart 11517; USGS Fenwick, Adams Run, Edisto Island, Bennetts Point.

BASE CAMP: Camping is not permitted on the NWR, but Edisto Beach State Park offers camping only 30 minutes away. Edisto Island also has resort accommodations and rental properties.

PUT-IN: From the Ashley River bridge in downtown Charleston, take US-17 S 11.5 miles to SC-162. Veer L and go 12 miles to SC-164. Stay straight on SC-164 and go 3 miles to SC-174. Cross the highway over to SR-55. Go straight 4.5 miles to the Willtown Bluff boat ramp.(You'll need to veer L at an unmarked fork in the road to stay on SR-55).

TAKE-OUT: Same as the put-in.

DAY TRIP: *Jehossee Island Exploration. This voyage takes you 16 miles around the southern half of the Edisto Unit of the ACE Basin NWR. Highlights are the remote wilderness location and the chance to observe the wide diversity of wildlife that inhabits the refuge. Difficulty rating: 2.*
    From the put-in paddle E on the South Edisto for 2 miles. The Dawho river appears to the N. Turn into the river and follow its winding route 4 miles to North Creek, which appears on the R. North Creek serves as part of the Intracoastal Waterway, so larger craft might begin to appear. Follow North Creek 3 miles back to the Edisto. Turn R and follow the Edisto 7 miles back up to the launch site. Stay close to the W bank of Jehossee Island to ensure you're going in the right direction on the windy Edisto.

Bear Island Wildlife Management Area

Bear Island encompasses the ACE Basin's southernmost holding that is accessible by car. In addition to a lack of roads, the lands south of Bear Island offer little firm ground for passage on foot, making them the remotest areas in the ACE Basin. The only way

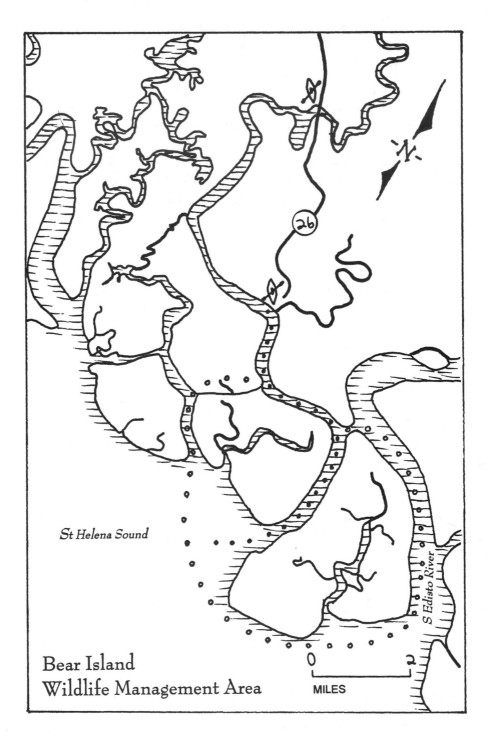

St Helena Sound

S Edisto River

Bear Island
Wildlife Management Area

0   2
MILES

to explore the region is by boat. Since the tidal creeks and flats which traverse the area have constantly changing depths, the shallow-drafted kayak is the perfect vessel for confidently roaming these waters.

And there is no shortage of space to roam. An extensive wetland dominates the landscape. Of Bear Island WMA's 12,000 acres, only ten percent are wooded. No trees can survive the harsh tidal environment. A few feet of tidal range drain or flood acres of land in just a few hours. The dominant flora are salt marsh species like black needlerush and cordgrass which thrive in this type of environment.

The abundance of water is consistent with the area's primary function as a waterfowl preserve. Managed impoundments support a wide variety of ducks. Birds such as cormorants, coots, herons and egrets inhabit these marshy lowlands. At elevations higher than the marsh, forested islands called hummocks provide habitat for other species. Notable migratory birds in the forested areas are the indigo and painted buntings, which offer colorful displays on their summer visits. Twenty-six breeding pairs of bald eagles inhabit the ACE. They often soar high above Bear Island.

Travelling the waters near Bear Island you're likely to encounter several of these species. The major artery in this part of the ACE Basin is the Ashepoo River, which roughly bisects the project's land. This river flows through the tidal waters along the banks of Bear Island before it empties into St Helena Sound. As you approach the sound, you'll notice new species of wildlife on both land and water. Look out for bottle-nosed dolphin which chase fish deep into the estuaries. These playful creatures do not shy away from kayaks. At low tide you might notice their ritual of hopping completely up onto muddy creek banks before sliding back into the water. Farther out to sea the endangered brown pelican is often seen gliding gracefully just above the water in search of a meal.

The beautiful blue ocean provides a welcome respite after paddling through acres of marsh. Strong shore winds provide refreshment and also keep the bugs off. The sandy beaches of Otter Island offer a nice place to set up camp for an overnight. The ability to camp here (permit required) means you can put together multi-day trips paddling the remotest sections of the ACE.

If you plan to paddle deep into the refuge, come prepared, because you're not likely to see anyone else. Be sure to bring plenty of water, sun screen, and insect repellant. When camping, make sure to practice the no-trace ethic in order to preserve the area for future visitors and wildlife.

INFORMATION: Bear Island WMA, Route 1, Box 25, Green Pond, SC 29446; 803/844-8957. There are no on-site facilities. Businesses are located along US-17 less than half an hour away.

MAPS: NOAA chart 11517; USGS Bennetts Point, Saint Helena Sound, Edisto Island, Edisto Beach.

BASE CAMP: Otter Island, part of the St Helena Sound Heritage Trust Preserve, allows camping when you obtain an advance permit from the South Carolina Department of Fisheries (803/795-6350). A primitive campground is available at Bear Island WMA by prior appointment. You'll find the closest hotel, motel, and B&B accommodations in Charleston or at one of the area's resort beaches.

PUT-IN: From its junction with US-21 follow US-17 N 14 miles to SR-26. Turn R and go 16 miles to the put-in at the end of the road.

TAKE-OUT: Same as the put-in.

DAYTRIP: *Sound Journey. A 12-mile trip down the scenic Ashepoo River to St Helena Sound. Highlights are the chance to observe a wide array of avian species and perhaps see bottle-nosed dolphin. Difficulty rating: 3.*

From the boat launch paddle the feeder creek until you reach the Ashepoo River. Follow the river S 5 miles to the St Helena Sound. You'll probably want to spend some time exploring the edges of this wide open sea. When you're ready to return, retrace your route back to the put-in.

WEEKENDER: *Otter Island Exploration. This 22-mile trip takes you on the Ashepoo and the Edisto, two constituent rivers of the ACE Basin. You'll also make a visit to the wide-open St Helena Sound and overnight on a remote barrier island. Difficulty rating: 4.*

From the launch paddle the feeder creek S a couple hundred yards into the Ashepoo River. Follow the river S 3 miles until the breach in Fenwick Island. Turn E through this short connector channel. Then turn S onto the Edisto and paddle 4 miles S. At the mouth of the Edisto bear W and paddle 2 miles to Otter Island. The front of the island offers hospitable places to camp on sandy beach.

On day 2 follow Otter Island around to St Helena Sound. Instead of going back up the Ashepoo, paddle NW 3 miles to Ashe Island. Enter the narrow channel on the island's E side. After 1.5 mile turn R into a small channel leading back to the Ashepoo and paddle for another 2 miles. Upon reaching the main channel turn N and paddle a 2 miles back to the launch.

Hunting Island State Park

Fripp Inlet ◊ Harbor River ◊ St Helena Sound ◊ Atlantic Ocean

Hunting Island represents one in a series of remote barrier islands that line the lower coast of South Carolina. While many of these southern islands encompass tracts of virgin beach front, Hunting Island State Park offers one of the few vehicle access points to this seaside wilderness. Area preserves, such as the ACE Basin (see separate entry above) and Tybee National Wildlife Refuge, protect fragile beachfront habitats by keeping them isolated from automobiles. In contrast to these more remote areas, Hunting Island State Park lands visitors right in the middle of a beautiful island preserve. This convenience gives kayakers the freedom to leisurely roam the surrounding waters without straying too far from base camp.

The coastal waters adjoining the park range from the wide-open expanses of the Atlantic Ocean and St Helena Sound to the protected waters of Fripp Inlet and the park lagoon. This diversity offers options to kayakers of all skill levels. Beginners often stay close to the lagoon where its calm, shallow water provides welcome protection from currents and swells. The maritime forest which borders the lagoon paints a beautiful backdrop for a peaceful float. The lagoon flows into Fripp Inlet which separates Hunting Island from Fripp Island. This inlet leads east to the Atlantic Ocean and west to the protected marshes behind the islands. These back barrier marshes contain an extensive network of feeder creeks that you'll likely want to explore. Experienced paddlers often venture north of Hunting Island to the open waters of St Helena Sound—one of the largest inlets on the southeastern coast. Its powerful currents wash the sand away before it can stabilize on shore. The result is a shoreline subject to rapid erosion and the most extensive shoals on the SC coast.

The neighboring inlet's powerful effect is apparent on Hunting Island. Walk along the beach and you'll notice the decaying

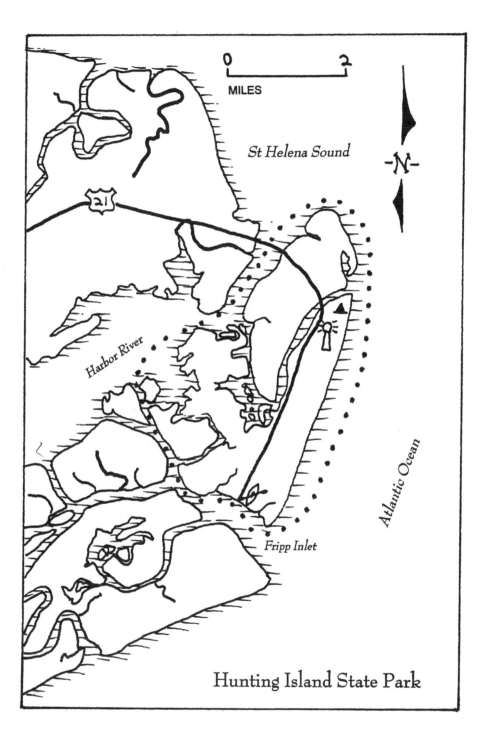

St Helena Sound

-N-

Harbor River

Atlantic Ocean

Fripp Inlet

Hunting Island State Park

stumps of live oaks washed over by tidal flow. The beach also lacks the dune fields that normally mark the transition between ocean and maritime forest. Longshore currents move the sand so quickly that the tides have flattened the dunes and advanced directly into the adjacent stands of trees. The island is losing approximately 15 feet of beach per year to erosion. Today the center of the island is most vulnerable while the northern and southern shores remain a little more stable.

While erosional forces have continually altered the island's profile during recent history, the northern end, where the lighthouse stands, traditionally has taken the brunt of the loss. Keepers of the lighthouse have moved the structure twice in the past 150 years. After the first lighthouse gave way to the encroaching ocean in the late 1860s, they built a new lighthouse on higher ground which incorporated design aspects that allowed for future relocation. In 1882 the northern end of the island experienced a four hundred foot, single-season loss to erosion. This amazing loss of beach forced keepers of the lighthouse to move the tower farther inland. In 1889 the lighthouse was moved to its present location, one and a quarter miles southeast of its previous dwelling. Although the lighthouse retired from active duty in 1933, the structure remains a popular visitor destination. The state park permits visitors to ascend the stairs which rise to breathtaking views. Although modern navigation doesn't rely on the landmark anymore, kayakers can appreciate the former significance of the beacon from the ocean.

Despite the encroaching sea, the park's 5000 acres encompass a highly evolved slash pine-palmetto forest where visitors can view large specimens of the state tree, the cabbage palm (palmetto), in its native habitat. Wildlife flourishes in this environment—the island's name derives from the successful game hunts that took place here. As a preserve, the island maintains large populations of formerly hunted species such as white-tail deer and raccoon. The park also hosts more than one hundred bird species that inhabit or visit Hunting Island.

These wilds likely account for the park's extreme popularity—Hunting Island State Park is South Carolina Parks and Recreation's most visited destination. This shouldn't deter adventurers seeking isolation, since crowds tend to congregate in the concentrated areas around the developed facilities. In any event, sea kayaking has a detectable presence on Hunting Island. In recognition of the sport's growing popularity in the SC lowcountry, the state park sponsors clinics periodically from late spring to early fall. The peaceful lagoon provides the perfect place to teach new skills to aspiring kayakers.

The park also offers five miles of hiking and developed camping. Predictably, the park beach is the most popular gathering spot among vacationers. Picnic areas also dot the park.

INFORMATION: Hunting Island State Park, 2555 Sea Island Parkway, Hunting Island, South Carolina 29920; 803/838-2011. A visitor's center at the SP has a basic map of the park and other free info. Water and restrooms are located inside. If you forget any essentials, a park store located near the campground's entrance has limited items. Phones are found at both the visitor center and the park store. A nominal parking fee is charged during the busy in-season. Park hours are from 6 AM–9 PM from April through September and 6 AM–6 PM from October through March.

MAPS: NOAA chart 11517; USGS Saint Helena Sound, Fripps Inlet.

HAZARDS: Though somewhat protected, the waters of the sound can get plenty rough on windy days. The open waters at the mouth of the sound are subject to unpredictable and sometimes dangerous currents. The deep waters around St Helena Sound attract larger boats.

BASE CAMP: Hunting Island State Park has a developed car campground with 200 sites. The sites cost $20/night. The nearest town with boarding is Beaufort which offers lodging and dining in a beautiful waterfront setting only 20 miles away. For more information call the Beaufort Chamber of Commerce at 803/524-3163.

PUT-IN: From its split-off with US-21 in Beaufort take Alternate US-21 S 21 miles to the Fripp Island Bridge. Just before crossing the bridge turn R into Russ Point Landing. Follow the dirt road until it dead-ends at the water. Here you'll find a small parking area and a boat ramp.

TAKE-OUT: Same as the put-in.

DAYTRIP: *Hunting Island Circumnavigation. This 14-mile circular trip takes you through scenic tidal marshes of inland estuaries and around the beautiful waters of St Helena Sound. Difficulty rating: 4.*

From the put-in follow Fripp Inlet 2 miles to Harbor River. Turn NE and paddle one mile through the wide open bay until it constricts to a narrow channel. Continue another 3 miles through this channel past Harbor Island to St Helena Sound. Spend some time exploring the sound if you like. The wide-open waters are a great place to test your paddling endurance and are a favorite haunt of bottle-nosed dolphins. From the northern tip of Harbor Island, follow its eastern beach front 6 miles across Johnson Creek and then along the shores of Hunting Island to Fripp Inlet. Turn W and paddle up Fripp Inlet. Less than a mile up the inlet, the tidal lagoon offers a nice diversion near the end of your trip. Its calm green waters are flanked by a tall maritime forest. Continuing along the inlet, you'll pass under the bridge and Russ Point Landing will appear on your R.

Pinckney Island National Wildlife Refuge
Mackays Creek ◊ Port Royal Sound ◊ Skull Creek

In contrast to the development on Hilton Head, Pinckney Island National Wildlife Refuge encompasses 4,053 acres of primitive coastal habitats located west of the large resort island. In fact, Hilton Head serves as a protective buffer between the refuge and ocean storms. The NWR plays a vital role in wildlife protection in the region. The sheltered haven it provides harbors endangered and threatened bird species which include the southern bald eagle, peregrine falcon, and wood stork. Although wildlife officials are primarily concerned with maintaining the habitats of these and other regional species, this wilderness incidentally provides kayakers with a beautiful and fascinating environment to explore.

Management practices at the refuge promote a diversity of species. The five freshwater impoundments allow many species to flourish on the refuge that wouldn't survive otherwise. Rookeries of snowy egret, cattle egret, tri-colored heron, night heron, and little blue heron take advantage of these ponds. Alligators, which prefer lower salt concentrations, nest around the impoundments. Nesting boxes for wood duck and platforms for osprey encourage these gorgeous birds to reproduce at the refuge. Other management practices include prescribed burning, selective cutting, and the planting of trees.

While these management practices have enhanced existing habitats, refuge lands already occupied a productive wetland environment. Two thirds of the refuge consists of salt marsh and tidal creeks, vital habitats to the maritime ecosystem. The estuaries and surrounding marshes spawn significant populations of fish, which in turn feed larger fish and mammals. Bottle-nosed dolphin often chase the spawning fish inland. Ebb tide brings raccoon, otter, and mink out into the marsh grasses to hunt stranded fish, crabs, and snails.

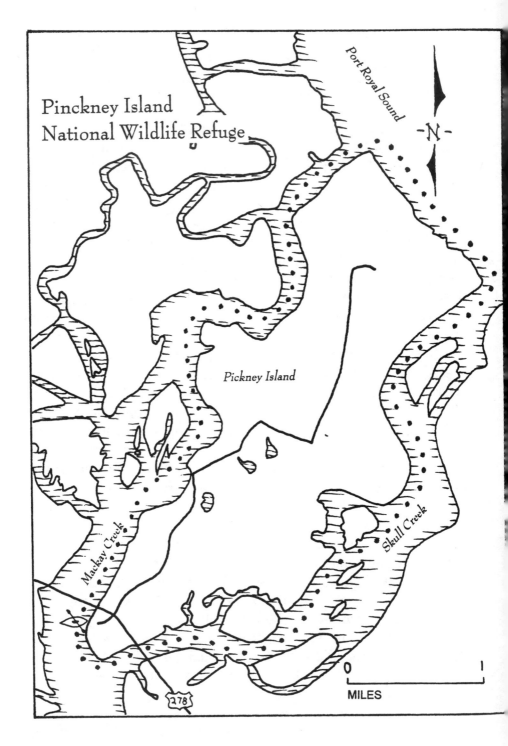

Pinckney Island
National Wildlife Refuge

Port Royal Sound

-N-

Pickney Island

Mackay Creek

Skull Creek

278

0   1

MILES

These nutrient-rich wetlands are fed by four inshore water-ways that merge at the refuge. Mackays Creek and Skull Creek form the western and eastern borders of Pinckney Island, and eventually converge at the refuge's southern end. Port Royal Sound and the Chechessee River join these creeks at the north end of the refuge. The web of estuaries gives kayakers plenty of options for exploring the neighboring refuge. The placid inland waters make for a peaceful float through the wilderness.

Lying within these waterways, Pinckney Island is the major landholding on the refuge. Neighboring Big Harry Island, Little Harry Island and Corn Island contribute smaller parcels of land. The land was once part of Major General Charles Cotesworth Pinckney's plantation. The revolutionary war commander successfully grew long-staple cotton in the area. In addition to his success as a plantation owner, Pinckney signed the U.S. Constitution and ran for president. The Pinckney family eventually sold the land which then became a major game preserve. In 1975 the property was donated to the U.S. Fish and Wildlife Service.

The refuge managers encourage low-impact visitation. Pinckney Island has 14 miles of nature trails accessible by foot or bicycle. These trails cover the many fascinating aspects of the refuge. Kayakers have the best perspective from the water, but landing on refuge lands from a boat is not permitted. The refuge is day-use only.

Other area attractions within a day's paddle are Calibogue Sound and adjacent Daufuskie Island. Pat Conroy describes Daufuskie in two novels, *The Water is Wide* and *The Prince of Tides*. The isolated island community is a nice spot to visit by kayak.

INFORMATION: The Savannah Coastal Refuges, Parkway Business Center, Suite 10, 1000 Business Center Drive, Savannah, GA 31405; 912/652-4415.

MAPS: NOAA chart 11516; USGS Spring Island, Parris Island, Bluffton, Hilton Head.

HAZARDS: What boat traffic there is in the area is concentrated on the Intracoastal Waterway.

BASE CAMP: Primitive camping is not permitted in the refuge. The popular resort of Hilton Head offers a variety of lodging options. Contact the Hilton Head Chamber of Commerce at 803/785-5577 Nearby Hardeeville on I-95 has hotel and motel accommodations.

PUT-IN: From its junction with US-21 near Beaufort, take SC-170 W 15.4 mi until you reach US-278. Turn L and go 15 miles to Pinckney Island NWR. The turn-off is located in a trough between 2 giant bridges. The boat ramp (C.C. High Landing) is on the R while the main entrance to the refuge is on the L .

TAKE-OUT: Same as the put-in.

DAY TRIP: *Circumnavigation of Pinckney's Island. This 12-mile voyage takes you around the main island of the refuge. Highlights include spying snowy white egrets in the marsh and dolphins frolicking in Port Royal Sound. Difficulty rating: 3 .*

From the boat ramp follow Mackays Creek, paddling NE under US-278. When you reach the expansive marsh of W Pinckney Island turn NW, aiming for the forested areas of Big Harry Island. Upon approaching the Harry Islands, turn E and travel along the forested regions of Pinckney Island. After a total of 4 miles from the put-in, Mackays Creek empties into Port Royal Sound. If you have time, enjoy paddling this wide-open expanse of water. Look out for dolphin, which often wander these warm waters. Follow the shoreline on the sound SE for a mile until you reach Skull Creek, which doubles as part of the Intracoastal Waterway. You might contrast the development E of Skull Creek to Pinckney Island's preserve. Follow Skull Creek 5 miles S back to Mackays Creek. The boat ramp is at this intersection.

Savannah National Wildlife Refuge
Savannah River ◊ Little Back River ◊ Salt Water Creek

The Savannah was once 238 miles of free-flowing river, beginning as a narrow trout stream in the North Carolina mountains and ending at a broad delta in the Georgia and South Carolina lowcountries. The river's length gave colonial settlers a convenient natural feature to designate the state line between SC and GA. The subsequent damming of major portions of the river severely shortened the distance that the mighty Savannah once flowed. Despite impoundments and other development, some beautiful riparian habitats still remain in a primitive condition.

Savannah River National Wildlife Refuge ensures that a significant portion of the lower river remains undisturbed. The refuge protects 13,000 acres of bottomland hardwood among its habitats. Cypress-tupelo forest once extended along all of the major coastal rivers in the southern Carolinas, but has been reduced to a few isolate patches over the past two centuries. This unique habitat supports wildlife that includes birds such as southern bald eagles, prothonotary warblers, and pileated woodpeckers, as well as larger animals such as feral hogs, bobcats, and American alligators.

In addition to the swamp forest, the 25,600-acre refuge protects significant tracts of freshwater marsh and tidal creeks and rivers. This wetland environment enticed early settlers to grow rice in the region. By 1850 13 rice plantations were located within present refuge boundaries. These former plantations have been converted into 2,800 acres of managed pools for migratory and wading birds. Remnants of the former plantations still dot the refuge. Two giant millstones symbolize the region's agricultural past. A seven-foot-deep cistern—an old device used to collect rainwater—also remains. Spanish moss-draped live oaks, which once fronted old plantation houses, have survived time better than the houses they adorned.

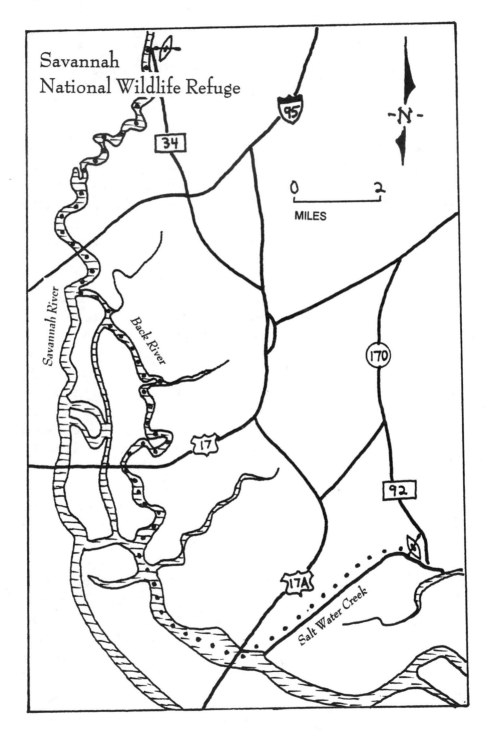

By kayaking the refuge you can see a mix of cultural and natural history. You'll travel from large stands of baldcypress through cleared impoundments and eventually into tidal river waters. This trip provides an excellent study in the gradual change of plant and animal species that accompany the different environments. While paddling the southern part of the refuge you'll notice several factories that line the Georgia side of the river near US-17. (Note: the suggested trip outlined below avoids a close encounter with these factories). Despite their unsightly appearance, the factories' proximity to such a sensitive, yet undisturbed, environment presents an encouraging example of the successful coexistence between industry and nature. Fortunately, you can avoid the factories altogether by carefully planning your trip.

Round trips are impossible on the upper parts of the Savannah NWR, since a fairly strong current exists this far inland. A lack of boat ramps in this area also limits your options for trip routes. The lowermost regions of South Carolina are very remote, making long trips the norm. Daring paddlers might attempt the arduous journey to Tybee Island NWR at the extreme southeastern corner of SC. Other one-way trips offer more promising possibilities such as the one described below. For shorter trips, you might kayak the creeks around the managed impoundments. This is a sure way to see wildlife, but limits the amount of paddling you can do. If you bring a rod and reel, you can fish these tidal creeks. This is a popular refuge activity

Besides paddling you might try a few land-based outdoor activities available on the refuge and environs. Twenty-five miles of hiking and bike trails interlace the refuge along the dikes in the managed areas. Laurel Hill Wildlife Drive allows you to witness part of the refuge via automobile. Nearby Savannah presents a beautiful Old South city where you can overnight while visiting the area.

INFORMATION: The Savannah Coastal Refuges, Parkway Business Center, Suite 10, 1000 Business Center Drive, Savannah, GA 31405; 912/652-4415. There's no on-site visitor center, but the Laurel Hill

Wildlife Drive on US-17, which is one mile E of the South Carolina-Georgia border, has an information signboard and pit toilets. No public facilities are located near the put-in, although the town of Hardeeville is near by.

MAPS: USGS Rincon, Hardeeville, Port Wentworth, Limehouse, Savannah, Fort Pulaski.

HAZARDS: The remoteness of the region poses the most serious hazard. To ensure you have enough time to arrive safely at your destination, leave early on your trip into this wilderness. To assist long paddles, time your trip to coincide with the tides.

BASE CAMP: Camping is not permitted on refuge lands. In Hardeeville, SC a host of inexpensive hotels are located at the junction of US-17 and I-95. These accommodations put you in the vicinity of both put-in and take-out. A larger variety of accommodations is available in Savannah, just a short drive from the wildlife refuge on US-17. For more information contact the Savannah Chamber of Commerce at 912/944-0444.

PUT-IN: From I-95, take exit 5. Turn N onto US-17 and go 0.7 mile to the junction with SC-46. Turn L and go 2.5 miles until the road, which becomes SR-31, dead ends into SR-34. Turn L and go 0.5 mile to the Mill Stone Landing on the R.

TAKE-OUT: Take US-17 (and then US-17A) from its junction with I-95 8.6 miles S to SC-170. After 2.2 miles turn R onto Shad Rd (SR-93), a 0.1- mile connector to Bellinger Hill Rd (SR-92). Turn R and go 2.2 miles to St. Mark's Baptist Church Rd (an unmarked dirt road). Turn R and go 1.3 miles to the put-in at the dirt landing Turn Bridge.

DAY TRIP: *Floating Down the Border. The first part of the trip traces the tupelo-cypress swamp along the state border and then explores the tidal marshes below the refuge. This long one-way trip covers 25 miles and requires two cars. Difficulty rating: 3.*

Try to plan your trip so the out-going tide occurs as you navigate the tidal section E of the US-17A bridge. From the boat ramp at Mill Stone Landing travel S on the Savannah. Follow its windy channel 7 miles, at which point the Little Back River splits off to the L. (I-95 serves as a landmark before the split). You'll encounter some of the 13,000 acres of bottomland hardwoods. Turn into the Little Back River and follow it S 12 miles on its winding course. At this point you are travelling through the heart of the refuge. You might notice alligators sunning themselves in the early spring months. They thrive in the freshwater marshes of the Savannah River and its tributaries. You'll pass under 2 more overpasses. After the second (US-17A), look for a breach in the marsh on the L which is Salt Water Creek. Follow this creek NE for 5 miles to the take-out.

Outfitters & Guides

The following businesses sell and rent sea kayaks and related equipment and/or offer guided trips. They are arranged geographically, from north to south, in a manner similar to the layout of the main part of this book. The only exception to this rule is that outfitters not located along the coast are listed from west to east in each state. We hope this makes finding a place to buy or rent a sea kayak as easy as possible. These businesses are included here as a service to our readers; the authors and Out There Press have received no compensation from any of them.

North Carolina

Bryson City
Nantahala Outdoor Center—13077 US-19W; 704/488-2175
Open M–Su: 8–5
Sales & Guided Trips

Hickory
Outdoor Supply Co—3006 N Center St; 704/322-2297
Open M–Th, Sa: 10–6; F: 10–8
Sales

Charlotte
Great Outdoor Provision Co—Park Rd Shpg Ctr; 704/523-1089
Open M–F: 10–9; Sa: 10–6; Su: 1-6
Sales & Guided Trips

Cornelius
Outdoors Etc—20212 Knox Rd; 704/892-1848
Open M–F: 10–8; Sa: 10–5
Sales

Winston-Salem
Great Outdoor Provision Co—Thruway Shpg Ctr; 910/727-0906
Open M–F: 10–9; Sa: 10–6; Su: 1–6
Sales

Greensboro
Pro Canoe & Kayak—1515 W Lee St; 910/294-3918
Open M–Sa: 10–6
Sales & Rentals

Durham
Great Outdoor Provision Co—Northgate Mall; 919/286-9201
Open M–F: 10–9; Sa: 10–6; Su: 1–6
Sales

Cary
REI—255 Crossroads Blvd; 919/233-8444
Open M–F: 10–9; Sa: 10–6; Su: 12–6
Sales & Rentals

Raleigh
Great Outdoor Provision Co—Cameron Village; 919/833-1741
Open M–F: 1—9; Sa: 10–7; Su: 1–7
Sales

Pro Canoe & Kayak—5710 Capital Blvd; 919/787-7720
Open M–Sa: 10–6
Sales & Rentals

Wilson
Adventure Bike & Trail—138 Parkwood Plaza; 919/243-6730
Open M–Sa: 9–6
Sales

Corolla

Kitty Hawk Sports—Timbuc II Shpg Ctr; 919/453-4999
Open Daily: 9–9:30 (hours vary seasonally)
Sales, rentals, Guided Trips

Outer Banks Outdoors—Monteray Plaza; 919/453-3685
Open M–Sa: 10–8; Su: 10–6 (hours vary seasonally)
Sales, Rentals, & Guided Trips

Duck

Kitty Hawk Sports—Winks Shpg Ctr; 919/261-8770
Open Daily: 9–9:30 (hours vary seasonally)
Sales, Rentals, & Guided Trips

Kitty Hawk

Kitty Hawk Kayaks—1/4 Milepost, US-158; 919/261-0145
Open Daily: 9–6 (hours vary seasonally)
Sales, Rentals, & Guided Trips

Nags Head

Kitty Hawk Sports—Milepost 13, US-158; 800/948-0759
Open Daily: 8:30–10:30 (hours vary seasonally)
Sales, Rentals, & Guided Trips

Kitty Hawk Watersports—Milepost 16, US-158; 919/441-2756
Open Daily: 8–11 (hours vary seasonally
Sales, Rentals, & Guided Trips

Outer Banks Outdoors—3933 N S Croatan Hwy; 919/441-4124
Open M–Sa: 10–8; Su: 10–6 (hours vary seasonally)
Sales, Rentals, & Guided Trips

Manteo
Outer Banks Outdoors—307 Queen Elizabeth Ave; 919/473-2357
Open M–Sa: 10–8; Su 10–6 (hours vary seasonally)
Sales, Rentals, & Trips.

Avon
Outer Banks Outdoors—39432 NC-12; 919/995-6060
Open M–Sa: 10–8; Su: 10–6 (hours vary seasonally)
Sales, Rentals, & Guided Trips

New Bern
Coastal Outdoor Outfitters—2703 US-70 E; 919/633-2226
Open M–F 9–6, Sa 9–5
Sales & Rentals

Ocracoke Village
Outer Banks Outdoors—Village Waterfront; 919/928-4563
Open M–Sa: 10–8, Su 10–6 (hours vary seasonally)
Sales, Rentals, & Guided Trips

Indian Beach
Island Rigs—1980 Salterpath Rd; 919/247-7787
Open M–Su 9:30–6 (summer only)
Sales & Rentals

Cedar Point
Waterway Marina Rentals—1023 Cedar Point Blvd; 919/393-8008
Open M–Su 7–6
Sales, Rentals, & Guided Trips

Jacksonville
Lewis & Clark Outfitters—1154 Western Blvd; 910/455-0678
Open M–F: 10–7, Sa: 10–6
Sales

Wrightsville Beach
Windsurfing & Sailing Ctr—275 Waynick Blvd; 910/256-9463
Open M–F 10–5, Sa & Su 10–6
Rentals & Guided Trips

Wilmington
Cape Fear Outfitters—1934A Eastwood Rd; 910/256-1258
Open M–F 10–7, Sa 10–6, Su 1-6
Sales, Rentals, & Guided Trips

Ships Store—7220 Wrightsville Ave;910/256-4445
Open M–Sa: 10–6:30
Sales

South Carolina

Travelers Rest
Sunrift Adventures—1 Center St & US-276; 864/834-3019
Open M–F: 10–7; Sa: 9–6; Su: 12:30–6
Sales & Rentals

Columbia
River Runner Outdoor Ctr—905 Gervais St; 803/771-0353
Open M–Sa: 10–6
Sales, Rentals, & Guided Trips

Cayce
Adventure Carolina—1107 State St; 803/796-4505
Open M–Sa: 10–6
Sales, Rentals, & Guided Trips

Florence
Naturally Outdoors—2195 W Evans St; 803/665-1551
Open M–Sa: 10–6
Sales & Rentals

N. Myrtle Beach
Wind N Sea Outfitters—803 28th Ave S; 803/272-4420
Open M–Sa: 10–6; Su: 1–5
Sales, Rentals, & Guided Trips

Georgetown
Black River Expeditions—21 Garden Ave; 803/546-4840
Open M–Sa: 9–5:30; Su: 1–5
Sales, Rentals, & Guided Trips

Pinopolis
Blackwater Adventures—1938 Pinopolis Rd;803/761-1850
Open Daily: 9–5
Sales, Rentals, & Guided Trips

Mt. Pleasant
Coastal Expeditions—514-B Mill St; 803/884-7684
Open Daily 9–6
Sales, Rentals, & Guided Trips

Charleston
Half-Moon Outfitters—320 King St; 803/853-0990
Open M–Sa: 10–6; Su: 1–5
Sales, Rentals, & Guided Trips

Canadys
Carolina Heritage Outfitters—SC-15; 800/563-5053
Open Daily 9–5
Sales, Rentals, & Guided Trips

Edisto Island

Cassina Point Outfitters—1642 Clark Rd (N end); 803/869-2535
Open By appointment
Rentals

St Helena Island

The Kayak Farm—1289 Sea Island Parkway; 803/838-2008
Open By appointment
Rentals & Guided Trips

Hilton Head Island

Outside Hilton Head—The Plaza at Shelter Cove; 800/686-6996
Open M–Sa: 10–6; Su: 12–6
Sales, Rentals, & Guided Trips

Coosawhatchi

Tullifinny Joe's—btw W Frontage Rd & I-95 & Tullifinny River
Open Daily: daylight hours   803/726-4545
Sales, Rentals, & Guided Trips

Index